THE HOUSE AT CHANNING AND MOONSAIL

THE HOUSE AT CHANNING AND MOONSAIL

A search for romance and meaning in the 70s and 80s

MARK ELLIS

LAURUS BOOKS

Unless otherwise notated, all Scripture references are from the New King James Version®. Copyright © 1982 by Thomas Nelson, Inc. Used by permission. All rights reserved.

THE HOUSE AT CHANNING AND MOONSAIL

BY MARK ELLIS

Copyright © 2021 by Mark Ellis

All rights reserved. This book is protected under the copyright laws of the United States of America. This book may not be copied or reprinted for commercial gain or profit. The use of short quotations or occasional page copying for personal or group study is permitted and encouraged. Permission will be granted on request.

Paperback: ISBN: 978-1-943523-74-0

Mobi (Kindle): ISBN: 978-1-943523-76-4

Published by LAURUS BOOKS

LAURUS BOOKS
www.TheLaurusCompany.com

This book may be purchased in paperback from: www.TheLaurusCompany.com, Amazon.com, and other retailers around the world. May also be available in formats for electronic readers from their respective stores. Available to booksellers at Spring Arbor.

"Never judge of the whole round of life by the mere segment you can see. The whole is, in the end, perfect."
—Frank Norris

TABLE OF CONTENTS

PART 1: BERKELEY BOUND 9
01 The Train to Berkeley 11
02 Deutsch Hall 15
03 Around the Dining Commons 19
04 Deep Throat 23
05 Forgettable Night 25
06 New Morality, New Politics 29
07 The Holidays 35
08 The Kidnapping 39
09 Ferragamo's Shoes 43
10 Harmon Gym 47
11 Change of Seasons 51
12 New Roommate, New Directions 57
13 Summer of '74 65
14 Reclaiming the House 69
15 A Blonde in Berkeley 73
16 Bunny From Texas 77
17 The Panty Raid 81
18 Seeing Ram Dass 85
19 Islander Party 89
20 Summer Road Trip 91
21 A Sophisticated Mountain Town 95
22 The Girls of Heardle Cottage 101
23 A Shocking Death 105
24 Spring Skiing with Dr. Dog 111
25 Home Again, and Then Off 115
26 Return To School 119
27 The Campaign of 1976 125

TABLE OF CONTENTS Continued

28 Boalt Hall Graffiti 129
29 Governing 133
30 The Sociology of Sports 137
31 Chapter Revolt 141
32 Skull and Keys 145
33 Woody's Talk 149
34 Awkward Endings, New Beginnings 153

PART 2: THE HOUSE ON MOONSAIL 157
35 Finding A Path 159
36 European Tennis Holiday, 1978 165
37 Relocation 169
38 In the Hunt 175
39 Surfing at Salt Creek 179
40 A Townhouse By the Beach 183
41 Salt Co. Ski Trip 189
42 The Presidential Campaign of 1980 193
43 Murder By the Sea 199
44 The Not-So-Great Debates 203
45 Becoming An Artist 213
46 Hunting For A Wife 217
47 Reclaiming Youth 221
48 Chance Meeting at Abramson's House 227
49 Reckonings 231
50 Palm Springs Weekend 237
51 The Ask 241
52 Wedding Bells 243
Epilogue 247

*Ellis family in the mid-1960s:
Donald, Mary Elin, Lisa, and Mark*

DISCLAIMER
This book is based on true events, filtered through 40-year-old memories. Names have been changed to protect the innocent and the guilty, the good, the bad, and the ugly …

PART ONE
BERKELEY BOUND

Mark 1973

CHAPTER ONE

THE TRAIN TO BERKELEY

Finally, the day I had been anticipating for months had arrived. It was the day I was to leave home for college. My parents dropped me off at the train station. It would have been a long day in the car to get to Berkeley from Rolling Hills, California. Plus, they had busy lives and probably had an engagement conflicting with my departure.

We arrived at Union Station in downtown L.A. on a bright and clear morning in early September 1973. I was wearing my favorite flared corduroy pants, pale orange flip-flops, and a colorful Hawaiian shirt, my usual attire, and lugged an old Samsonite hard-shell suitcase and an extra box filled with clothes and a few other items.

I had learned to surf that summer and had become a surf "Nazi," going almost every day, rain or shine, so my long, curly brown hair was bleached mostly blonde. I spent so much time in the sun and had such a deep tan that my aunt derided me by saying, "You look like a Mexican!" when she saw me.

I also taught tennis that summer on a court in our backyard, earning extra money for school. My parents were covering the $212 per quarter tuition, but I had to buy my own books and cover incidentals like beer.

Accompanying me on the train journey was a high school acquaintance, Jack Beatty, who had also been accepted to Berkeley. After a casual conversation one day in our senior year of high school, we decided to room together in the dorms. This morning, we both found ourselves together on the train.

Beatty resembled the Moondoggy character in *Gidget*, actor James Darren. In his junior year of high school, he managed to buy a sleek white MGB GT and attracted a Jewish American princess for a girlfriend. He was a tall, handsome, wise-cracking rebel who often came to school quite loaded.

In his approach to life, he was Jack Nicholson to my Art Garfunkel in the film *Carnal Knowledge*, light years ahead of me when it came to sex, drugs, and rock music. I figured that by rooming with him, I might coast into some interesting situations on his coat tails, especially with the opposite sex. I must confess that I was a bit disappointed when he did not take his car to school, but I think he may have sold it to pay for his schooling.

As we pulled out of the station, I could not help but think about my paternal grandmother, Reta Jane Cooper, who had arrived at the same station in 1913, some 60 years earlier. She and her family came out to California from a farmhouse in Long Point, Illinois, where her grandfather, John Cooper, homesteaded following his service in the Civil War.

After Grandma Reta and her family arrived in downtown Los Angeles, they went to live at her uncle's 10-acre orange ranch at the corner of Sunset and La Brea in Hollywood, right across the street from Charlie Chaplin's studio.

Grandma Reta remembered playing with a little girl who was in the movies, a diminutive budding starlet who had regular dancing and music lessons. When Reta Jane was invited up to her friend's room and saw all of the pretty dresses in her closet, she thought she had entered a fairytale land. She did not believe anyone could lead that kind of life.

After they stayed at her uncle's place for a while, Reta's father decided

CHAPTER ONE
THE TRAIN TO BERKELEY

he would homestead 160 acres in Anza, east of Los Angeles. Unfortunately, the property had very poor soil that would not produce a crop, and they almost starved.

After they had built a modest house, they ran out of money. The family basically lived on her father's pension from the Spanish-American War, $12 a year. "Twelve dollars a year was almost unthinkable," she told me, "but we didn't need to buy gasoline, and there were no taxes to pay. We just had a team of horses and lived a very simple life." They seldom had meat on the table. Vegetables were scarce or of poor quality. They mostly ate biscuits and bread, with some Crisco gravy on top, browned with a small amount of flour and raw milk. They also had eggs from a few chickens and a couple of cows and pigs. Such was life in southern California in the early part of the 20th century.

On the other side of L.A., my maternal grandfather, Rod Gomes, lived in Chavez Ravine. He was the 13th of 15 children born to Edward and Minnie Gomes. Coincidentally, the Gomes family also moved to California from Illinois, preceding my grandmother's family by 24 years.

With so many children gathered around the dinner table, Rod's father kept a buggy whip handy to enforce discipline. If any of the kids complained about their food, they were sent to bed immediately. To save money and feed that many mouths, they ate soup almost every night. Rod was sent to the local butcher in the afternoon to fetch a bone for the soup. When the butcher saw Rod enter his shop, he said, "Here comes Soup Bone." That ten-cent soup bone fed a family of 15.

"Please give me a bone with plenty of meat on it," Rod always requested.

The Gomes boys were good at baseball. One of Rod's brothers played professionally in Denver, and another played for the Chicago Cubs. Rod played in the Pacific Coast League until he got hurt. In 1927, he went to work at the docks as a longshoreman for 80 cents an hour. Later, when the Depression hit, they cut his pay back to 65 cents an hour.

Grandpa Rod's favorite TV character was Archie Bunker. He related strongly to the character with the racist, anti-Semitic views and overall approach to life. I remember watching TV once with him when Barbara Streisand came on. He started ranting and raving, cursing at the 20-inch black and white screen. Similar invective was leveled against the occasional African Americans who appeared on television in those days.

His big hero was the longshoremen's union leader, Harry Bridges, who was nearly deported because of his communist sympathies. In those days, everything at the docks was lifted by hand. Grandpa Rod worked the night shift for most of his career, so shortly before our train pulled out of Union Station, Rod was climbing into bed after a full night's work.

The train left the station slowly and moved through the concrete wasteland, but as we continued north, the ride had a beautiful section as we chugged along the aquamarine coastal waters south of Santa Barbara. The seas were calm with about a three-foot swell wrapping gently around one of the points. Then turning inland, it became somewhat monotonous until we went through some wooded terrain in the north.

When the train stopped in San Jose, a woman got on that bore a strong resemblance to Alice B. Toklas. She was dressed head to toe in black, walking through the train from one car to another, bearing a large silver platter of brownies, which she was giving away to anyone who might indulge. Jack and I both ate a brownie, and by the time we departed the train in Oakland, we were both flying about as high as the well-lit Campanile Tower on the Berkeley campus.

* * * * * * *

CHAPTER TWO

DEUTSCH HALL

A yellow taxicab deposited us at our new home, Deutsch Hall, a 10-story carbuncle of a building named after a classics professor. The architecture might have been at the cutting edge of modernity in 1960 when it was constructed, but it already gave off a stale, dated look. We found our room on the second floor and discovered we were the first on the floor to arrive.

The room had a Spartan simplicity, one rung above San Quentin, with two single beds, two dressers, and two very simple wood desks.

In the laundry room, there was a Coke machine. I put a quarter in the slot and suddenly, the machine started dropping cokes like we hit a jackpot in Las Vegas. Every drink in the machine fell out and we were scrambling to grab them and run them over to our new dorm room. Soon, the entire contents of the machine were lined up on a closet shelf.

To decorate and personalize the drab interior, we made a quick trip to a head shop on Telegraph Avenue filled with imported items from Central Asia, where we found floral bedspreads from India and a giant M.C. Escher black and white poster of reptiles crawling out from a printed page. Jack also picked up a miniaturized bong he called a carburetor, meant to draw marijuana smoke more deeply into the lungs. He also happened to have some seeds, so we began growing weed in five-gallon plastic containers on pallets we took from a loading dock. Soon our den of hedonism and iniquity was taking shape.

From our broad window on the second floor, we could watch the new arrivals walking into the complex. Some arrived with parents and others came solo. Frankly speaking, most of the females arriving at Berkeley in 1973 were mostly brainy feminist types who refused to shave their legs or armpits and wore combat boots.

Jack and I immediately noticed two exceptions to the foregoing. One was Kim Schultz, an overly tan country club girl whose father was an executive with a large liquor company. The other was Heather Lange, who arrived from Sacramento wearing overalls, with long straight silky hair and a gorgeous face that could adorn the cover of *Outdoor* magazine.

The guys arriving on our all-men's floor, for the most part, came ready to party. Beer and marijuana seemed to be everywhere. Soon we were passing joints around in a room at the end of the hall occupied by Ben Craig from San Diego, a mischievous, fun-loving hippie prankster with Jesus-hair that fell to the middle of his back and a bushy beard. He appeared to be older than the rest of us, while I was barely shaving.

One night, I went down to Ben's room, and he had placed towels around the crack of the door and somehow filled the room with pot smoke. He and his roommate, Jason Chang, were cavorting about in the smoke-filled haze, with Ben wearing a breathing apparatus that looked like a World War I gas mask, which allowed him to maximize his smoke inhalation. We were having a wild time with the music cranked up when we heard a knock at the door.

It was Jason's father, a short Asian man who almost got knocked over by the whoosh of smoke that blasted him when the door opened. Scowling and barking at the same time, he demanded that Jason come out of the room. We soon learned that Jason would be moving in with a different roommate down the hall.

In the room next door to us were two guys from Sacramento,

Don Oster and Beau Brogger, whom we began to call *Brick*. Don, the son of a real estate developer, did not join in with the party crowd very much. When I went over to borrow something from him one day, I noticed he was studying intently a list of all the members of the U.S. Senate and memorizing their names. He was undoubtedly a political animal, destined to run for office some day.

His roommate, Beau, was entirely different. One night, we woke up after midnight, and Beau was yelling out his window, obviously drunk. All the sound and fury of a group of inebriated soccer hooligans seemed to be channeled into one brain and one roaring mouth.

"Hey, shut the f___ up!" we yelled over at him. "Don't you know what time it is? Get to bed, asshole, and sleep it off."

The next morning, his roommate, Don, knocked at our door with a somewhat grave expression on his face.

"Hey, guys. I've got to warn you about Beau. Don't mess with him when he's been drinking."

We had noticed Beau was physically imposing, a former linebacker with a broad chest, covered front to back with thick hair, a gap between his front teeth, and a crazed Neanderthal look in his eyes when he was loaded. He had wavy, dirty blonde hair that fell to his shoulders.

"The summer after his junior year, Beau got in trouble," Don continued. "He was drinking in a park along the American River with friends when a policeman came up and confronted them. Beau beat up the policeman and had to spend a summer in a work camp."

After absorbing this news, we were a bit more cautious around Beau, not wanting to set off any volcanic eruptions.

There were parties every night until school started. At one of the pot parties in Ben's room, we passed around joints in a circle, then after we took a hit, we were supposed to write something pithy in a small journal being circulated. I scribbled something and signed my name, but it was apparently illegible because when Ben attempted to read the various jots and tittles, he couldn't make out my name and yelled out "Loomis!" He mistook Ellis for Loomis, and soon everyone on the floor had adopted that as my new nickname.

Registration involved turning in computer punch cards that were fed into giant mainframe computers that filled an entire room. Weaving my way through the drug-filled haze, I felt some anxiety bubbling up as I wandered among the stately buildings on campus, wondering if I would be able to cut it with all these brainiacs in one place, especially the Asian students who never seemed to party or slumber in their determination to bury the rest of us academically.

* * * * * * *

CHAPTER THREE

AROUND THE DINING COMMONS

The food in our dorm complex was a long way from Chez Panisse, a little restaurant in the neighborhood that had recently opened. Instead of Alice Waters' inspired interpretation of California Cuisine, we slogged through Cafeteria Cuisine with titles like Waikiki Meatballs, featuring a gelatinous glowing yellow sauce swimming over extra-fatty, mini ground beef balls, pineapple chunks, and sticky white rice.

It was not long before we learned about a streaking epidemic at a college in Texas. Not to be outdone, the word spread one night at dinner that we would take up the challenge of running naked around the outside perimeter of the dining commons. So, after enough beers to shed our inhibitions and clothing, except for a ski mask, Jack and I joined the rowdy group of exhibitionists racing through the cool night air, exposing our shortcomings, to the raucous cheers of a huge throng of spectators from the dorms.

A few days later, I had my first lunch at Heather's table with her Sacramento cohort. I was immediately smitten by her untamed beauty and ridiculously profane speech, punctuated by high-pitched giggling squeals.

Suddenly, her hot dog and beans were the source of every possible joke about the male anatomy. Every punch line involved penises and got her laughing almost uncontrollably. I had never been around such a beautiful, uninhibited woman.

After lunch, I followed her over to the women's dorm, which was identical to the men's dorm. Downstairs, in a large common area, there was a piano. Heather sat down and began to play songs from Joni Mitchell's *Blue* album.

Her head and long silky hair swayed as she sang,

> *I wish I had a river so long*
> *I would teach my feet to fly.*
> *Oh, I wish I had a river*
> *I could skate away on ...*

Suddenly, I felt like Graham Nash, drawn by the seductive charms of a rare talent, releasing something inside of me that seemed dangerous and unpredictable.

Heather turned out to be a *Star Trek* fanatic, so we found ourselves in a crowded room after dinner watching reruns of the series on a small black and white TV. The room was elbow to elbow with engineering students, budding computer geeks, and sci-fi fans enamored with the space opera revolving around Captain Kirk on the starship USS Enterprise.

Later, in Heather's room, we found ourselves alone, laughing, and having fun with each other. I was so intimidated, however. I thought she was probably out of my league, so I was being cautious about diving into romance too soon. She asked me to turn away at one point as she changed her top, exposing her breasts in front of me, as I closed my eyes part way and squinted, so as to catch a fleeting glimpse through my eye lashes of her well-formed chest.

Since the food in the dining commons left so much to be desired, we often made late-night runs to Top Dog, a tiny hot dog stand on Durant Avenue north of Telegraph that could accommodate about 10 people

CHAPTER THREE — AROUND THE DINING COMMONS

squeezed around a large grill filled with every variety of sausage, cooked to perfection. Often, it was the only possible answer to the late night urges that came from the over-consumption of cannabis and the yawning void left by the cafeteria.

* * * * * * *

CHAPTER FOUR

DEEP THROAT

Jack and I heard the D.K. Theater in Berkeley was showing the movie, *Deep Throat*, which had become a cultural phenomenon. Suddenly, it was chic for celebrities and upper middle class people to view explicit porn, and they were streaming in to see Linda Lovelace seek romantic advice from her psychiatrist, played by Harry Reems, who made the fascinating discovery that she had a rare genetic mutation that misplaced her clitoris in her throat.

After we agreed to go see it one night, Jack began to voice concerns about running into fellow classmates in the theater or its immediate vicinity.

"What if we go in disguise?" I suggested. He quickly agreed, and somehow we put together trench coats, fedora hats, and dark glasses that made us look like Chicago mobsters. We trooped down to the D.K. on Telegraph Avenue, a theater that had only recently taken over a Sprouse Reitz pharmacy.

It was a rainy night, and we made a mistake about the starting time and arrived late. The theater had some deferred maintenance, so there were buckets in the lobby catching rainwater from a leaky roof. The roof was so bad they closed off the main entry door to the theater, and we found ourselves walking in through the front.

As my eyes adjusted to the darkness, I could see a packed theater, which seemed to be disproportionately filled with Berkeley professors—unmistakably the leftist elite—with long graying hair and beards, round spectacles and tweedy jackets, diligently absorbed in this latest extension of the sexual revolution.

There was no other way to get to two empty seats than to walk across the front of the stage, so we plowed right ahead, but it happened to be at a very climactic point in the storyline, involving close-ups of sensitive anatomical territory. As we walked in front of Linda Lovelace's private parts, partially blocking the audience's view, there were howls of protest from many who had only recently been raising hell over America's involvement in the Vietnam War.

I had never seen explicit pornography in film. I first viewed *Playboy* magazine at a friend's house in 1965 when I was ten years old. In those days, the front, nether region of a woman's anatomy was not shown, but carefully hidden by the clever photographers employed by *Playboy*'s founder, Hugh Hefner. After my first view of *Playboy*, I was hooked, and had built up a collection of pages I clipped from throwaways and kept hidden in my bedroom at home.

But seeing explicit, hardcore porn on the big screen was shocking. I made love for the first time with my high school girlfriend in the back of a VW Squareback, outfitted with Hawaiian curtains made by my grandmother, but this was really more than I could handle. In fact, it seemed more revolting than alluring.

The next morning, Jack woke up with testosterone overload, and he leaped out of bed and began to parade around the room in a tee-shirt and nothing else, chortling with glee as he displayed his anatomy in the fetid air, his crimson face aglow with fiendish delight, like the Joker come to life.

* * * * * * *

CHAPTER FIVE

FORGETTABLE NIGHT

Every Friday and Saturday night, Jack and I would buy a six-pack apiece, and he would supply the marijuana. After dinner, we sat in our darkened dorm room and cranked up the Allman Brothers or some other group in our combined collection of albums. We seemed to both have similar tastes in music, which helped our relationship.

Led Zeppelin, The Doors, The Who, Jethro Tull all made the list. As we pounded beers, and he lit up his mini-bong to inhale deeply of the psychoactive weed, one song that became an anthem of sorts was *"Whipping Post,"* recorded live at Fillmore East. We sang along with Gregg Allman's soulful, bluesy vocals as he reached the crescendo,

> *Sometimes I feel, sometimes I feel,*
> *Like I been tied to the whippin' post.*
> *Tied to the whippin' post, tied to the whippin' post.*
> *Good Lord, I feel like I'm dyin'.*

One night, one of our high school friends came over from Stanford to party with us. Erik Fleischman could only be described as "the prince" of Miraleste High School, coming from a wealthy, prominent family that Jack and I compared to the Kennedys in terms of their prominence in our community.

Erik's father, James, had built a conglomerate in New York that owned a number of prominent companies. For several years, James was always listed in the Top 10 of the highest paid executives in the U.S., and it seemed astonishing to us that he commuted from Rolling Hills to New York by private jet. Jack was in awe of the family and talked about how James had been number three in his class at an Ivy League school, "behind a Jew and a woman," and that he had such a demanding schedule that his entire day was carefully divided into 15-minute increments.

Starting in junior high, Erik was always chosen as president of the class. He eventually got to Stanford on a baseball scholarship and was in a pre-med program. His wild side, which we saw plenty of in high school, was in rare form with us that night. The more loaded we got, the more boisterous we became until, at one point in the evening, Erik let out a howl, jumped up in the air, and punched a hole through one of the ceiling tiles in our dorm room with his fist.

After that, we made our way to some of the parties in the frat houses. Usually, the fraternities had a keg of beer, liberally spilled and splashed throughout the immediate vicinity, with people standing around drinking out of red plastic Solo cups.

I met a mousy freshman student named Ginnie at one of the parties and somehow ended up spending the night at her place. As the bright morning light flooded into Ginnie's dorm room, I woke up next to her with a hangover, barely remembering how I got there.

When I looked at her, I was stunned. She appeared relatively attractive in the darkness the night before, but the harsh light of morning was less kind. Her complexion was pale, her hair thin, disheveled, with brownish curls, and crooked, decaying teeth overdue for dental attention. I couldn't help thinking, *How did I end up in bed with one of the least attractive women on the Berkeley campus?*

I began to miss my high school girlfriend, Laura. Tall, slender, blonde,

CHAPTER FIVE   FORGETTABLE NIGHT

and beautiful. *How could I have let her go?* I broke up with her after my high school graduation, feeling the need for independence as I went off to college. She stayed behind for her last year in high school. I was probably too cavalier in the way I handled it, and I know she was deeply hurt. The girls at Berkeley were nothing like Laura. I had a big crush on Heather, but she seemed unattainable.

I grabbed a piece of paper and a pen that lay near the bed and began to wax poetic ...

> *Gliding madly under fireball skies*
> *the joker and I*
> *cringe at violet plumes*
> *that twist and contort*
> *our speeding bodies.*
> *We are caught*
> *lost undefinable*
> *feel emerging sunrises*
> *Great jumping time warps*
> *we rush past into night*
> *Caravan of steam gleaming flesh*
> *no moths on the radiator*
> *stardust caught between my teeth*
> *and the joker laughs*
> *No hard driving*
> *stand up comic*
> *wheeling dealing used car salesman*
> *could sell me a vehicle to eternity*
> *So here we all are*
> *caught in a rush*
> *the crimson-faced joker and I*
> *two fly-by-nights in death.*

I got a letter from Laura in response to one I sent to her. I had seen her momentarily at the first football game of the high school season, right before I left for Cal on the train.

Dear Mark,

It made me feel really good to hear from you. It was strange, I just knew that today I'd get a letter from you. I don't know if I even understand what was going on in my head at that football game. I hadn't seen you in a long time, and I'd missed you, and I wanted to talk to you. I thought maybe we could talk that night, but then you said you were going out to dinner with your parents, so I knew I'd have to say goodbye after the game.

I was feeling kind of screwed because I wanted to know what you were feeling, and I wanted to touch you and for you to hold me and say everything's all right, but none of it was happening.

I've been going to a psychology class with Jamie on Thursday nights. It's an adult class, so I'm the youngest one there. Last week, we had a speaker on sensuality that was really great. I might have a chance in the near future to have a strange kind of experience. Jamie always goes to this nudist colony up in Topanga Canyon, and she said I could go if I wanted to. I was planning on going this weekend, but my mom thinks some dirty old man is going to rape me, so I don't know if she's going to let me go. I hope she does because Jamie was telling me that they do tribal massage and stuff like that. I think I could really get into it.

I've been going out just about every weekend. Oh, well, maybe things will shape up soon. Tell Jack I send him my love, and don't you guys get in too much trouble.
Love,
Laura

* * * * * * *

CHAPTER SIX

NEW MORALITY, NEW POLITICS

On Sunday night, after a weekend of solid partying, I trudged over to Moffitt Library where most freshman students studied. I divided my time between Moffitt and studying in my room.

I was alarmed when I opened my books and began trying to recall my studies from the previous week and drew a blank. I could not seem to remember anything from my classes or homework. Was it true what they said about marijuana affecting the short-term memory? The thought was unsettling. My roommate Jack had a steel-trap mind and could manage the heavy partying without any apparent repercussions.

I was scared for the first time in my life about the approaching midterms and finals in this relatively short 10-week quarter system. I hit on an ingenious solution in my mind: cheating, something I had never resorted to in high school. But the pressure I felt from all these stellar minds in one place and the fear of failure drove me into the arms of ethical compromise.

Admittedly, my moral compass was not well-formed. Neither of my parents had any church background nor devoted any time to instructing about ethics and morality. My dad came from a broken home. His father,

Carl, left his mother, Reta Jane, for a secretary. His maternal grandfather had been suspicious of religion and steered my father into the agnostic camp. As a child, I asked dad if he believed in heaven and hell, and he said, "I've come to believe that people make their own heaven or hell on earth."

My mother grew up in a home with parents who should have divorced. They fought all the time and slept in separate bedrooms. My grandmother slept with her door locked. When Grandpa Rod came home from working at the docks during the night shift, after a few bumps at the Prop Room in Wilmington with the guys, he would yell and curse outside her door in a threatening manner. Sometimes he would sharpen knives in close proximity to her bedroom, which heightened the emotional toll on her.

So neither of my parents had a church background, but because it seemed like it might be a good thing to do, they took my sister and me to the First Presbyterian Church in San Pedro as children. As we got older, we went to church less and less. I never darkened the door of a church in high school.

My parents were socialites and mostly let us raise ourselves, without a lot of coaching or instruction about life. Because of the homes they grew up in, I don't think they had been parented much themselves.

In my first midterm, I found myself in Harmon gym with several hundred other freshmen. They told us to bring our own "blue books," thin notebooks about 20 pages long, for the exam, so I jotted down notes in one of the blue books as reference material for the exam and used the notes during the exam.

The cheating, the heavy partying, the casual sex all gave me a vague unease that was brushed off with the idea, prevalent at the time, that a new morality was emerging of situational ethics, unmoored from the rusty, worn-out traditions of the past.

"If it felt good, do it" was the thought, as long as you weren't hurting someone else. "Go for it" was another popular slogan in my high school. "Get naked!" was the raucous cry at our parties.

I narrowly escaped an unnerving encounter with religion in the

CHAPTER SIX — NEW MORALITY, NEW POLITICS

summer after I graduated from high school. One night a member of the high school tennis team invited me to his Baptist church in San Pedro, where they had a visiting evangelist. This guy was a classic stem-winding southern preacher, and he scared me about two topics I had not given much thought about—sin and judgment. When the altar call came at the end, I was sweating profusely and felt compelled to go forward, but my heart wasn't in it.

I went home that night, opened my collection of *Playboy* clippings, and indulged my fleshly appetites. The good old devil seemed to have his hooks in me, and that wasn't going to change anytime soon.

My roommate Jack was also very opposed to Christianity. As we were taking bong hits, he would deride people he knew in high school that had become Christians.

"John Stinson was one of the best football players on our team, and after he became a Christian, he turned into a pussy," Jack declared. "Christianity took the fight out of him. It makes you weak; only people who need a crutch turn to that."

He had recently read Eric Hoffer's *The True Believer*, which informed his view about religious people he considered "fanatics," people who were frustrated or insecure about their own lives who joined churches as an escape from themselves.

* * * * * * *

I grew up in a Republican household, but my parents did not talk much about politics, and I was very apolitical. But since 1968, I had been aware that the winds of change had been swirling in the air, and America was not the same place portrayed in the television shows I grew up with.

On Monday, October 22, 1973, I grabbed the campus newspaper, *The Daily Californian*, as I walked to class. The headline, "Nixon Dismissals Spark Outrage," spoke to the uproar created when President Nixon fired Special Prosecutor Archibald Cox and Deputy Attorney General William

Ruckelshaus.

Elliot Richardson had resigned on Saturday night rather than fire the two, but after Robert Bork became the acting attorney general, he carried out Nixon's order to dismiss them.

The secondary headline read: "Watergate 'Compromise': Demos Talk Impeachment." While Nixon's lawyer, Fred Buzhardt, rejected the talk of impeachment, there were reports of possible mass resignations from the Justice Department. *Could Nixon really be impeached over this?* I wondered.

A staff writer for the *Daily Cal*, Steve Ross, called it the "worst crisis since the Civil War," and an impeachment rally was scheduled that night by the ad hoc "Citizens Committee to Impeach President Nixon." One of the history profs on campus was quoted in the paper, asking, "Can the President get away with criminal acts?"

Nixon had Quaker roots in Whittier, California, and my grandfather remembered trading at the Nixon's store and seeing young Richard around. He seemed to have strayed a great distance from his early Quaker beginnings.

The Ellis side of my family were all Quakers going back to Wales in the 1600s when Rowland Ellis, the owner of a farm known as Bryn Mawr, heard George Fox speak in Dolgellau and became an ardent follower of the movement.

But he and other Quakers were heavily persecuted by the Church of England, with fines levied, jail time, even horses confiscated because the Quakers refused to tithe to the Church, among other supposed crimes.

In a letter to his cousin written in 1675, Rowland Ellis described meeting the founder of the Quaker movement, George Fox, at the Quaker's annual meeting. Rowland described Fox as "a big man, of such pallor as bears testimony to his long imprisonment. He has the long, fine nose of an aesthete, a broad mouth, and eyes that pierce through one. I can well understand why a man once cried, 'Turn those eyes away,' as he felt that look upon him."

By contrast, my ancestor described seeing William Penn at the same meeting, "whose appearance was vastly different from that of the rest of us. I was surprised at the richness of his clothing. His silk waistcoat stood out against the greyness and sobriety of our attire. Round his neck he wore a collar of delicate lace and ruffles of the same material at his wrists. His hair was longer and more fashionably tended than ours, and his whole demeanor indicated that he belonged to the gentry. His voice was the first thing that struck me. Its tone was cultured, accustomed to speaking the poetry of Milton and the prose of Jeremy Taylor."

Yet, Fox and Penn had been united by their shared sufferings on behalf of Quakerism. "Hast thou heard how Penn has been jailed time and time again, the last time at Newgate, that most cruel and most filthy of prisons?"

Both men had been imprisoned at the grimy facility. "George Fox spoke of the opportunity he had in Newgate (prison) to propagate the Gospel of Light among the other prisoners. Not a word about his all too obvious suffering—only gratitude to God for such a valuable opportunity. Listening to him I felt certain that there was a troubled time ahead of us. But ... we must make the most of adversity. Through our suffering, others will find the solace of everlasting love ... For our part we must increase our witness and use our persecution to grind the mills of God."

Elsewhere, Rowland wrote about "the light which illuminates the secret room of the heart."

What is this light he wrote about and how does one find it, I wondered. *And why were my ancestors so willing to endure persecution and suffering for the sake of this light?*

* * * * * * *

CHAPTER SEVEN

THE HOLIDAYS

I did not go home for Thanksgiving, which seemed like a long trip for just a few days, so I accepted an invitation from Heather to spend the holiday at her house in Sacramento with her and her mother.

Her mother reminded me of my favorite fourth-grade teacher, with her broad face, pear-shaped, sturdy body, and kindly manner. Heather never mentioned her father much, and I ascertained her parents had been divorced.

The first night at her house, I did something idiotic. After a much-appreciated home-cooked dinner, we talked for a while and went to bed.

I could not get to sleep and found myself, instead, overcome with a sense of wild desire toward Heather and mounting sexual frustration. I got up from my bed and crept into Heather's dark bedroom. Her door was open, and I could tell by her breathing that she had fallen asleep already.

Somehow, in my mind, I thought I could quietly slide into bed with her. We would start cuddling and nuzzling, mutual romantic feelings would emerge, and everything would be groovy. Such were the imaginings of an 18-year-old, THC-laden mind.

As I edged closer to the bed, she awakened with a start, sat up on an elbow, and said, "What are you doing?" with alarm.

"Uh ... uh ... I don't know." I turned around sheepishly and slunk out of the room.

The following day, at breakfast with Heather and her mother, I came up with a lame excuse that I was sleepwalking, something I had done in my childhood. As I dug myself deeper, embellishing the lie, I had a nagging feeling from their wide-eyed reaction that they weren't buying it.

At the Christmas break, renamed Winter Break so as not to offend anyone's sensibilities, I went home for the first time in a couple of

Mark and Lisa 1974

months. It was amazing to me how much had changed in a relatively short time.

My sister, Lisa, presented a growing challenge for my parents because, at 13, she had fully developed into a beautiful, voluptuous young woman, attracting the wrong kind of attention from older guys who only seemed to have one thing in mind.

My parents were pretty conservative folk. They were apolitical registered Republicans and didn't discuss politics much at the dinner table. In 1965, they heard Ronald Reagan speak at a local restaurant and came home like the fishermen who had seen Jesus for the first time.

"We hope he runs for office!" they declared. "We would vote for him for anything." Considering their conservatism, it was a wonder they had sent me off to Berkeley, the home of the Free Speech Movement and a locus for protests against the Vietnam War, some of which had become quite violent.

However, when I first trudged through Sather Gate into Sproul Plaza in the Fall of 1973, the war was winding down, and the protests were subsiding. I drew a very high draft number and had no chance of going to Vietnam.

I was a lover, not a fighter. I had never been in a fistfight in my life, and I had never played Army as a kid. I certainly could not imagine myself ever being trained to kill "the enemy" in jungles halfway around the world. The testosterone-driven warrior spirit had seemingly bypassed me. If I had drawn a low number a few years earlier, would I have gone? The question plagued me.

I reconnected with my high school girlfriend while I was home. Oh, how I had missed Laura, who suddenly seemed more beautiful than I remembered, with her stunning figure, wavy thick blonde hair, and fair complexion. In light of the sparse opportunities at Berkeley, I had begun to reconsider my hasty decision to break up with her.

When I picked Laura up in my tan VW Squareback at her home in Portuguese Bend overlooking Marineland, I was already high. She started giggling when she realized it, and my effervescent, goofy, comedic side emerged as we cruised down Pacific Coast Highway.

After dinner, we drove past her house on Narcissus Lane, pulled over at the end of her dark street, and steamed up the interior of the car.

* * * * * * *

CHAPTER EIGHT

THE KIDNAPPING

Back at school for the Winter Quarter, I experienced my first northern California winter, which wasn't as bad as I expected because the state had entered into a drought cycle, meaning less rain. The cool air was bracing as I walked to school, and if it began to rain, I had a poncho that sufficed.

On February 5th, 1974, I awakened to the startling news that a fellow student, Patty Hearst, the 19-year-old granddaughter of newspaper magnate William Randolph Hearst, had been kidnapped from her apartment three or four blocks away from where I lived.

At about 9 PM the night before, Hearst's boyfriend, Steven Weed, answered the doorbell of their apartment, and three members of the Symbionese Liberation Army (SLA) burst in with guns drawn.

They beat up Weed, bound Hearst, threw her in the trunk of their getaway car, and sped off to a house in Daly City, south of San Francisco. Locked in a closet for weeks, she suffered extreme deprivation, abuse, and rape until she succumbed to the Stockholm Syndrome and joined their cause.

I was shocked by the popular support for the SLA in Berkeley. Posters began to spring up around town lauding them as heroes. Founded by Donald DeFreeze, aka Field Marshall Cinque, the group had already gunned down Oakland Schools Superintendent Marcus Foster, using hollow-point bullets packed with cyanide. Even though Foster was the first black superintendent, the SLA labeled him a fascist because of his plan to introduce I.D. cards in Oakland schools.

Cinque grew up in a home in Cleveland with an abusive, violent father who broke his arms as punishment. He ran away from home, lived with a fundamentalist minister for a while, then joined a gang. He spent the next few years in and out of prison, usually for stealing. An early probation report described him as having a "schizoid personality" and an unusual fascination with guns and explosives.

At Vacaville Prison, a visiting African American linguistics professor from Berkeley began to influence Cinque with leftist thinking through a program known as the Black Cultural Association. Cinque broke away and formed his own group, which became the genesis of the SLA.

After Hearst's kidnapping, the SLA began to communicate through the media to the authorities, and they always signed their missives: DEATH TO THE FASCIST INSECT THAT PREYS UPON THE LIFE OF THE PEOPLE. Jack and I liked the slogan so much we began spouting it to each other at times when we were high and needed a declarative punch line for our twisted ripostes.

On April 15th, 1974, we were shocked to discover Hearst had joined ranks with the SLA under the moniker "Tania" (the *nom de guerre* of Che Guevara's comrade) and was involved in robbing the Hibernia Bank in the Sunset District of San Francisco. Security cameras caught her toting an M1 rifle, barking orders to bank customers, two of whom were shot during the heist.

The *San Francisco Chronicle* splashed a photo of her slender, shadowy figure inside the bank on the front page of the paper. Could this be the same art history student who had grown up in a mansion in Hillsborough? Only recently, she had been on a private art tour of the great museums in Athens, Venice, Florence, and Rome, cultural "enlightenment" for a

CHAPTER EIGHT

THE KIDNAPPING

future life of privilege.

She was labeled a "common criminal" by the U.S. attorney general and found herself indicted by a grand jury for robbery, even though there were some reports that two of the SLA members kept their guns trained on Hearst during the entire affair.

The SLA soon demanded that two of their members, jailed for the killing of Marcus Foster, be released. They changed their revolutionary tune when that was not happening, demanding that Citizen Hearst give $70 of food to every poor person in California. Some estimated that would amount to about $400 million. Surprisingly, the Hearst Corporation made arrangements to give away $2.0 million as a first tranche, with trucks delivering food parcels to pre-arranged distribution centers.

In West Oakland, only a few miles from the Berkeley campus, five thousand people showed up at the distribution point. It turned into a debacle, with people storming the trucks, fighting each other, and throwing food parcels from the back of the vehicles to a seething mob. There were many injuries in the melee, with some needing hospitalization. In the America of fruited plains, could there be that many people so desperate for food?

* * * * * * *

After the kidnapping, I got a letter from Laura in the mail:

Dear Mark,

It's kind of hard for me to even start writing because I don't know if I should be. But I figure I can't keep everything inside, I have to let it out sometime. I've been feeling really down lately because I haven't heard from you in almost a month. I can reason that you've got other things that are keeping you busy, but then I think that you don't care about me, and it hurts.

It's really difficult to express my feelings because I'm afraid of being rejected, but I guess I trust you to understand. I don't know if I should be writing you because I feel like I'm bugging you or something. But I need to know how you're feeling, not thinking, but feeling deep down. I need to feel close to you. Oh, I'm feeling screwed right this minute.

I feel better since I've written down what's inside me. I'm not going to read it over again because I probably wouldn't want to mail it if I did. I'm afraid because I've put my feelings on the line, and I don't know what you're going to think.
Love,
Laura

* * * * * * *

CHAPTER NINE

FERRAGAMO'S SHOES

I made the decision to attend Berkeley primarily because it was the only University of California campus with a business major at the time. It seemed incongruous that the epicenter for radicalism in the state (and country) had the only business program. Even though I loved history first and foremost, I was persuaded by my father's success in business to pursue something that seemed more "sensible" for landing an actual job.

After dad's parents divorced when he was seven-years-old, there was no money. His mom, my Grandma Reta, worked as a schoolteacher in Costa Mesa, California, and schoolteachers were severely underpaid in those days. So starting at about age 12, Dad went to work as a soda jerk at Pink's Drugstore in Costa Mesa, then worked setting pins by hand at the bowling alley on the Newport peninsula. Some smart aleck decided it would be funny to send a ball rolling while Dad was still setting up the pins, and it went crashing into his knee, which caused a weakness in that knee the rest of his life.

Dad worked his way through Santa Monica City College and then UCLA loading baggage for United Airlines. He married my mother and landed his first job after college, selling computers for Sperry Rand-Univac. At that time, computers were larger than a Cadillac convertible.

One of his accounts for Univac was a guy named Ray Fawkes with Financial Secretary, a small financial services company that had begun to use data processing to help people with their monthly budgeting.

Fawkes somehow persuaded Dad to come and work for him, and Dad became his "fair-haired boy." Ray began to groom him to one day take over the company, or so it seemed.

That didn't sit so well with one of Dad's fellow co-workers, Wayne Hughes, an extremely sharp, aggressive, and ambitious young man already putting in 15-hour days to further his and the company's success.

One day, Wayne was startled to read an article in a business magazine about a young graduate from USC, Cal Johnston, who had already become a millionaire in real estate with his company, Property Research.

This is crazy. How is that guy making all that money, Wayne wondered, beside himself with curiosity and envy.

Wayne picked up the phone and called Property Research and asked who was in charge of hiring. When they transferred the call to the woman in charge, Wayne boldly pronounced, "I think I should come in and meet you because I'm going to be coming to work for the company."

She set up the appointment, but inwardly was fuming. She stormed into VP Walter Burns' office, and said, "I thought you told me you were never going to hire another person without me having an opportunity to comment on it."

"I didn't do it; I didn't hire him," Burns protested. "What's his name again?" Burns thought for a moment and said, "The only person who could do that is Cal Johnston."

So Burns went into the president's office and asked, "Who is this guy, Wayne Hughes, that you hired?"

"I never heard of him …"

"Well, he's coming in for an interview and said he's coming to work here."

Johnston paused for a moment, with a bemused look on his face. "I would like to meet that guy when he comes in."

Hughes and Johnston met a few days later and Johnston was enamored. "Okay, well, I want to hire you," he told Hughes. "How much do I have to pay you?"

"Whatever you think I'm worth, that's what you have to pay me."

Johnston named a figure and hired him on the spot.

The company grew rapidly selling real estate partnerships as tax sheltered investments. One year, they outsold Coldwell Banker, earning double the commissions of the better-known entity.

Wayne went to visit Dad and persuaded him he should get into real estate and paved the way for an interview. With Wayne's recommendation, Dad was hired and quickly immersed in the go-go world of high-flying real estate sharpies making multi-million dollar deals across the country.

Dad went from making $9,000 a year in his previous job to earning close to $100,000, which bought a few steak dinners in the sixties. He traded in our Ford Falcon and acquired a sleek, powder blue Buick Riviera and took up the habit of smoking cigars on his long commute home from Beverly Hills.

By the time I left for Berkeley, Property Research had blown up due to an SEC investigation related to the company's aggressive practices, selling real estate as securities for tax shelter purposes. What they were doing was legal, but the government didn't completely understand it, so they suspended their operations during the investigation, which killed the company.

Wayne departed the company and started Public Storage, which grew

Donald Ellis working at Property Research

into a behemoth, making him a billionaire.

Dad also left to start his own real estate company with a former Arthur Anderson CPA, Richard Lane, and the two of them were already off to a good start, creating partnerships to buy apartment buildings and industrial properties. Dad's unusually rapid ascent from hardscrabble beginnings created an aura around him in the rest of the family, and I wanted to follow in his footsteps, not realizing we had very different wiring.

As a result, I majored in business, and one of the core requirements was a class in calculus. It was much tougher than any math I had encountered in high school, and sitting in the midst of a class of about 100, I often felt lost.

Vince Ferragamo, Cal's freshman quarterback sensation, happened to be in the same class. When Ferragamo entered the classroom, with his girlfriend in tow, it was as if Zeus and Athena dropped in from the clouds. He had thick, wavy dark hair and strong chiseled features.

But the remarkable aspect was his girlfriend. She actually dressed like a woman! There were no combat fatigues, hairy legs or armpits. No Berkeley boots, Birkenstocks, or Earth shoes. She wore a short, tight-fitting tan skirt and hose, with matching stacked heel pumps and a billowy white blouse. Her blonde hair gently curled beneath her shoulders. Where did she come from? Why were there no other women remotely resembling her on campus?

Later, we were disappointed to learn that Ferragamo was transferring to Nebraska. "He didn't want to stay around here with half-filled stadiums," Jack told me. It was true. The residue or radicalism still permeated the atmosphere of Berkeley, and that caused a dampening effect on people's enthusiasm for football.

"Ferragamo wants to go to a place where they worship football, like Nebraska. There, he'll have 100,000 screaming fans filling the seats and putting him on a pedestal." I couldn't argue with Jack, but I couldn't help but wonder what it would be like to walk in Ferragamo's shoes.

* * * * * * *

CHAPTER TEN

HARMON GYM

To stay in shape for surfing, I decided to start swimming laps at the pool next to Harmon Gym. It was a decrepit old facility built in the thirties that had massive concrete walls surrounding the pool, giving off vague hints of Albert Speer's New Reich. But the walls funneled the sunlight and created a shield from the wind, so you could swim throughout the winter months with relative warmth.

In swimming laps and surfing, I had to overcome a childhood fear of water and ocean waves, one of my most embarrassing secrets. When I was five-years-old, mom took me to Adlai's Swim School near my grandmother's house in Palos Verdes. I didn't want to go in the water, so the owner picked me up and threw me into the deep end. The trauma that resulted from that ill-conceived idea scarred me for several years, so I didn't learn to swim until I was 12, very late for kids in Southern California.

After I learned to swim, we went to the beach as a family. I stayed close to the shore while Dad went out body surfing in the larger waves. He saw me piddling around with the tykes in the shallows and said, "Come on out, it's great!" He was a naturally strong, confident swimmer. The swimming coach at UCLA wanted him for the team, but he was too busy working to entertain the thought.

With Dad's encouragement, I trudged out toward the bigger waves. Then a large set of waves came through, and I got knocked over and tumbled around like a loose sock in a spin cycle. I came up sputtering and gasping for breath, with a newfound fear of large ocean waves. In swimming laps and learning to surf at 17, I mostly overcame my anxieties, but a latent fear of large waves stayed with me.

I soon discovered that Harmon Pool and Gym were favorite meeting spots for homosexual men. In the restroom, there were holes bored through the metal walls between the stalls. As I sat on the toilet one afternoon, I glanced over and noticed an eyeball peering lustily through a jagged hole.

"Ugggh!" I groaned, jamming a piece of toilet paper into the opening. I left hurriedly, completely unnerved by the experience. My sheltered upbringing in suburbia left me completely unprepared and ignorant of such things. In my youth, "homo" was a pejorative term thrown around without much thought as to what it really meant. Frankly, I had no idea such a world existed.

A few weeks later, a note was dropped into my locker from a secret male admirer, inviting me to make a connection. I showed it to Jack, and he laughed.

"This is what you get for hanging out down there," he retorted. Jack was philosophically opposed to weight lifting or swimming laps, lumping them both into the category of "bodily improvement."

"Only fags are into that sort of thing. I would avoid the place."

In the next few weeks, Jack and I started visiting fraternity houses. Dorm life was getting old, and he thought frat life seemed attractive, even as it had fallen out of favor to a large degree in the late sixties, with some houses even shutting down.

Jack seemed to be drawn to the Beta House, which was filled with studly-looking jock types from affluent families in Pasadena, Orinda, Piedmont, and other bedroom communities in California that populated Cal's Greek system. I followed along on Jack's coattails, even though I didn't seem like much of a fit in the jock house.

My three athletic passions, surfing, skiing, and tennis, along with my lean build, did not put me on an equal plane with the guys always chosen first on the playground for football teams.

Jack's Type A personality and incisive wit allowed him to be a consummate schmoozer at fraternity keg parties. I hung back a bit, but after a few beers, I could usually rise to the occasion. Still, I was almost always in the shadow of Jack's outsized personality.

We connected with Brock Hogan, the guy who seemed to be in charge of "rushing" new prospects for the Beta House. He came from a well-connected family in San Marino, California. His mother's side of the family held the Spanish land grant for Santa Fe, New Mexico, so he spent holidays there.

Another frat we visited had been used a couple of years earlier as a shooting location for the film, *The Graduate*, starring Dustin Hoffman as Benjamin Braddock, an awkward leading man if there ever was one. The Theta Delta Chi house at the corner of College and Durant, right across from my dorm complex, had the sort of classic, ivy-covered walls that made it perfect as the residence of Elaine's boyfriend Carl in the film.

Jack and I had one classmate from high school so enamored with the movie, probably wanting to emulate Benjamin's unlikely sexual prowess, that he bought a red Alfa Romeo Spider convertible, identical to the one driven by Benjamin in the film. Accepted to Berkeley, he drove the car up Highway One on his way to campus to recreate a famous scene in the movie. Later, we learned he dropped out of Berkeley, probably because real life could never match the fantasy constructed by the great film auteur, Mike Nichols.

As we toured the Theta Delta Chi house, we learned that one of the stars on Cal's football team, Chuck Muncie, was a member and happened to be upstairs. "He's too coked-up to come downstairs right now," one of the frat brothers informed us. We had seen Muncie run. He was like a runaway locomotive or wild stallion that could not be stopped or tamed, running over people, carrying players who could barely bring him down.

Was cocaine the secret sauce that propelled his frenzied activity on the field, or was it something deeper in his psyche? Later, we discovered that Muncie had grown up poor, one of six children in Uniontown, Pennsylvania, a steel and coal-mining town that had been the site of violent battles between workers and management. In one case years earlier, guards armed with machine guns faced down 1500 striking workers. In the ensuing melee, five were killed and eight wounded.

He grew up in a home with a disabled father, so his mother ran the show. His father used different spellings of Muncie to avoid bill collectors.

At six years old, the future footballer was hit by a truck, breaking his leg, hip, thigh, and arm. Doctors put him in a full body cast for six months and informed his parents he would probably never walk normally again. The accident left one leg shorter than the other, so he compensated by wearing an extra-thick sole on one foot. Growing up in a home surrounded by many relatives who had worked in the mines, he saw the effects of black lung and some who sustained serious burns in the steel mills. Athletics was his only ticket out of Uniontown, and Muncie, along with three of his brothers, had enough talent and drive to punch that ticket out of town. I began to understand why Muncie ran with such a fury, and it seemed to go well beyond the drugs.

The fraternity I liked the best, Phi Gamma Delta, or Fiji, didn't have as many jocks. They actually had lost their house due to some riotous excesses in the late sixties, so they were living in an old two-story boarding house on Durant Avenue. Most tours of frat houses were not very impressive, with the senses overwhelmed by the smell of beer, piss, and dirty socks. But these guys kept a pretty clean house, and they tended to compete with each other to have the coolest room to impress females.

* * * * * * *

CHAPTER ELEVEN

CHANGE OF SEASONS

After going through the motions of exploring fraternities, I got some stunning news from Jack toward the end of the winter quarter.

"I'm transferring to UCLA," he announced one afternoon.

"No ... say it ain't so," I said, reeling from the news.

"Berkeley just doesn't have what I'm looking for," he continued, as he explained that Berkeley had fallen short of his expectations about campus life, largely fostered by an older friend who regaled him with stories about beautiful women, wild parties, and the athletic prowess of Cal's sister school to the south.

I had grown up rooting for UCLA football and basketball because my parents met there. I was drawn to the school myself but chose Berkeley because of the business major.

I fully bought into my parents' side of the crosstown rivalry between USC and UCLA. UCLA's quarterback, Gary Beban, was my childhood hero. His last second heave into the end zone to win the USC game, known as the "Beban bomb," was the stuff of lore in our household. Mom and Dad happened to be at a restaurant in L.A. and saw Beban shortly after he won the Heisman Trophy. They came home with a cocktail napkin bearing his autograph. I was floating in the clouds for a week. John Wooden's basketball teams were also highly venerated.

So I felt a bit of envy about Jack's transfer combined with the painful prospect of losing my social cohort, someone I leaned on rather heavily for relational connectivity. I went home for spring break feeling dejected, unsure what the remainder of my first year would bring.

At home, my parents were still very involved with their social lives that revolved more and more around the Jack Kramer Tennis Club in Rolling Hills Estates. They took up tennis in their early thirties and had since become avid players, my mother particularly. She had never been athletic before age 30 but had suddenly become a very good player, inheriting the hand-eye coordination from the professional and semi-pro baseball players in the Gomes family tree.

They built a tennis court in our backyard, and she took a lesson and played almost every day. It became a healthy obsession that earned her a national ranking in her forties, playing against the elite of women's tennis in senior doubles competitions, women like Dodo Cheney, the first American to win the singles title at the Australian Championships.

In the summer of 1971, we had traveled up the freeway to the L.A. Tennis Club to watch the Pacific Southwest Championship match between Pancho Gonzales and Jimmy Conners. Remarkably, Gonzales at age 43 defeated the 19-year-old rising star in three sets by playing on the baseline, instead of his regular serve and volley style.

Conners used an aluminum Wilson T-2000 racket that was unlike anything ever used before or since. Among the pros, Conners was the only prominent player to master its unique stringing pattern that created a trampoline effect, adding power to Conners' service returns and smashing forehands. My parents bought me one, and I took to it, but using the racket set one apart as slightly odd because not many could adapt to its use.

The son of a house painter in Los Angeles, Gonzales grew up in a relatively comfortable middle class home. His given name was Ricardo, and he was called Ricardo or Richard by family and friends but was given the nickname "Pancho" or "Gorgo" by fellow players. "Pancho" was a common ethnic slur of sorts used for Mexican-Americans at the time. "Gorgo" was short for gorgonzola, the Italian cheese, and undoubtedly someone's sharply barbed mispronunciation of Gonzales that stuck among the players.

Gonzales was a physical specimen, standing 6 feet 3 inches tall and weighing 183 at his prime. His forehand was once clocked at 112 miles per hour, the fastest in tennis, and he could cover the court like a panther.

To add to the mystique, Gonzales had a mean-looking scar that ran across his left cheek, rumored to be the result of a gang-related knife fight. Nothing could be farther from the truth. The scar actually came from an accident on his childhood scooter when he was 7.

Gonzalez competed with a chip on his shoulder and a fierce, brooding presence that could intimidate lesser mortals. I talked to ball boys that were assigned to his matches and came away shaken after he spit or cleared his horse-like nostrils on them.

Part of his anger and resentment stemmed from the fact that, early in his career, he was often paid less than players he could beat. Prior to the arrival of the open era of tennis in 1968, players were compensated on a contractual basis. Tony Trabert, for example, was under contract for $80,000 a year in 1956, but Gonzales was contracted at $15,000, even though he usually beat Trabert.

Gonzales' overpowering serve and volley game became so dominant for a time that, incredibly, the rules on the pro tour were changed to prohibit a player from taking a volley immediately following his serve. The new rule, meant to thwart Gonzales, stated one had to wait for the ball to bounce after the return, rather than take it in the air. The folly of such a ridiculous rule soon became apparent, and the original rules were reinstated.

Jack Kramer, a bitter rival, once observed that "the majority of players disliked Gonzales intensely."

His stamina was also the stuff of legend. In Wimbledon at age 41, Gonzales played in the second-longest match of all time against Charlie Pasarell, 16 years younger than the fading star. But Gonzales prevailed in an epic 5-hour, 12-minute match with a final score of 22–24, 1–6, 16–14, 6–3, 11–9. Their marathon helped provide the impetus for the tie-breaker rule change that shortened the game.

When we saw Gonzales play in L.A., he had recently relocated to Las Vegas as the Tennis Director at Caesars Palace. The geographic pairing made sense to one *Sports Illustrated* writer, who noted: "There was no more perfect match than Pancho and Vegas: both dark and disreputable, both hard and mean and impossible to ignore."

Gonzales and marriage were not a great fit, as he had six failed attempts that produced nine children. His final wife was the sister of Andre Agassi, and it turns out Gonzales' father-in-law hated Gonzales so much that he considered hiring someone to bump him off. Pancho Segura once cracked, "You know, the nicest thing Gorgo ever says to his wives is 'Shut up.' "

Sadly, Gonzales died at age 67 from stomach cancer, his tennis winnings exhausted, with few friends, and estranged from his ex-wives and children except for Rita, his last wife. There wasn't enough money left in his bank account to pay for his funeral. In a remarkable display of grace and class, tennis champion Andre Agassi picked up the tab for the service.

I hung around the Jack Kramer Tennis Club starting in high school, which made me feel like an outsider because many of the young tennis stars had been playing there since they were very young, groomed by pros like Del Little and, later, Robert Landsdorp.

The club was set in gently rolling hills punctuated by low shrubs and eucalyptus trees on the Palos Verdes Peninsula. The parking lot was heavily populated with top of the line American cars, a few sleek Mercedes, and an occasional sports car. But Rolling Hills was not as flashy as Beverly Hills, for example, and the one-story, ranch style homes on a half-acre or more with barns and horses understated the level of affluence.

Beneath the veneer of respectable conservatism, there were a few dark secrets known by some of the old-timers at the club. For example, one rising young star's parentage was not what it seemed to be. She was actually the love child of her mother's secret, torrid affair with a tennis pro, who took the young protégé under wing and gave her a lesson almost every day, assuring her future success on a wider stage.

At one of the club's Tony banquets, some of the teenage tennis punks came to me with a plan to steal a case of champagne from the bar set up near the pool. They asked me to be their getaway driver. I agreed to the plan and soon found myself hauling them and the case of the bubbly in my VW Squareback, speeding through the hills to an uncertain destination. They got cold feet, insisted I drop them off, and I found myself with the purloined alcohol, which I hid in the attic in our garage.

One afternoon, I went up to grab a bottle and lost my grip. It fell about 10 feet onto the concrete floor and exploded, with glass shards and the wafting effervescence everywhere. I knew my parents were coming home soon, so I did what I could to clean it up, but the smell was overpowering. When I heard the garage door open, signaling their return, I locked myself in the bathroom and jumped in the shower. Soon I could hear my mother pounding on the bathroom door.

"What happened in the garage? Were you drinking out there? What in the world happened?"

I sheepishly related a story about spilling a little bit of wine and narrowly wriggled my way out of the situation without any serious repercussions. They had a remarkably light disciplinary touch with me based on my good grades and squeaky clean image, while their concerns about my sister absorbed the brunt of their punitive measures.

* * * * * * *

CHAPTER TWELVE

NEW ROOMMATE, NEW DIRECTIONS

When I returned from spring break, I opened the door to 205 Deutsch Hall and was met by an unexpected sight. My new roommate had taken it upon himself to rearrange the furniture, so now the two beds were pushed together, end-to-end, and he was laying on one of the beds wearing only white jockey shorts and a baseball cap, reading a book.

"Hi. I'm Jerry," he volunteered nonchalantly.

"I'm Mark ... good to meet you. I see you've made yourself at home."

"Well, I decided to change a few things ... do you like it?"

I lied and said I thought it looked okay. He was about my height, five feet eleven, with a slender build, lily-white skin, pencil-thin arms, and piercing eyes. His straight, ash-blonde hair falling below his cap gave him something of a Dutch boy look.

Since Jack and I both wore boxers, the sight of Jerry in his tighty-whiteys was jolting.

He immediately noticed I was wearing a Hawaiian shirt and began to laugh. Coming from northern California, he was not familiar with the surf culture of the southern climes, and immediately associated my fashion statement with former President Harry Truman, in his mind a hayseed in the world of fashion. He got a big laugh out of my choice in shirts.

I introduced him around, and we heard there was a Bruce Lee movie, *Fist of Fury*, showing at Bowles Hall. We trudged up to Bowles, the first residence hall built at Cal in the twenties that resembled a medieval Gothic castle built out of stone. A projector was set up in the living room of the all-male bastion, and about a hundred guys were hooting and hollering as we watched Lee fly through the air, punching and kicking his way to Kung Fu glory, always overmatched but victorious.

In the film, based in Shanghai in the early 20th century, Lee as Chen Zhen defends the honor of the Chinese against Japanese aggressors. In his first fight he beats back about a dozen Japanese single-handedly using a nunchaku as a weapon during the fight.

There was one topless scene in the film, and Jerry turned to me unexpectedly and whispered, "She has good boobs, huh?"

The summer before I arrived at Berkeley, Lee died suddenly and unexpectedly at the age of 32, what doctors officially labeled "death by misadventure." It seems he was in Hong Kong to have dinner with actor George Lazenby, the youngest actor to ever play James Bond. Before dinner with Lazenby, he was in the apartment of an attractive Taiwanese actress, Betty Ting Pei, "going over scripts."

About 7:30 pm, Lee began to complain of having a terrible headache, and Ting gave him Equagesic, which contained aspirin and a tranquilizer sometimes called Equanil or Miltown. Lee went to lie down and never woke up. Producer Raymond Chow came to the apartment and tried to rouse him unsuccessfully, summoned an ambulance, and Lee was declared dead on arrival at Queen Elizabeth Hospital.

An autopsy found his brain had swollen from 1400 to 1575 grams, which experts later stated was due to an allergic reaction to the tranquilizer in his system. One strange twist in his untimely death is that Lee had his underarm sweat glands removed in 1972 because he didn't think his soaked clothing looked good on film. This may have caused

CHAPTER TWELVE — NEW ROOMMATE, NEW DIRECTIONS

Lee's body to overheat while practicing his fighting techniques in hot weather, resulting in heat stroke that aggravated the cerebral edema that led to his shocking and untimely death.

A couple days after we went to see Lee's film, a letter arrived in our postal box addressed to "Kim Novak." I only knew one Kim Novak and that was the statuesque blonde actress Hitchcock made famous in *Vertigo*. I wondered if I should open the letter or return it to the postman? A funny feeling came over me ...

I went into a stall in the restroom, opened the letter, and began reading. My heart began to race. It was a torrid and explicit love letter from Jerry's boyfriend in Santa Barbara. How could I have gone from an alpha male roommate resembling Jack Nicholson to Kim Novak in a few short weeks? I decided I wouldn't let on I knew anything about Jerry's sexuality, but suddenly I realized his comment about boobs and the *Playboy* pinup next to his desk were meant to create a false impression, and that he wanted to keep that part of his life a closely guarded secret.

A few days later, I went up to Strawberry Canyon to hang out at the swimming pool and ran into Kim Schulz, the liquor company exec's daughter. Jack had tried to get something going with her, but never made it very far. I cornered her at one end of the pool, got within about six inches of her wet face, and breathlessly spilled my guts about the letter, seeking her advice. She was about as mortified as I was and clueless about the homosexual world.

"You can't really do anything," she said. "I'm sure he probably wants to keep things a secret, so you probably don't have to worry about it."

With my social world turned upside down, I fell headlong into the arms of the Fijis, who invited me to a beach day in Santa Cruz. From my home in Southern California, a trip to the beach was a relatively short 15 or 20-minute drive. But to get to anything resembling a good beach from Berkeley required a two-hour drive. They picked a warm spring day, and as we loaded up the car for the drive, Maria Muldaur's lilting tune, "Midnight at the Oasis" was wafting out of someone's window in the Fiji's rented boarding house.

After the beach day, I accepted an offer to join their frat, which would mean going through initiation before the end of the school year. Part of the appeal of joining them was the fact that they would be moving into their old abandoned house at the top of Channing Circle.

It seems a Bekins van had shown up in front of the three-story brick mansion in the spring of 1968 and started moving the furniture out. Everybody was kicked out, and an armed guard was placed on site to enforce the matter.

All the fraternities were dying in the late sixties. The Fijis didn't have enough pledges (recruits) to stay afloat financially, and their alums didn't want to subsidize them. The boys had also been in disfavor with the university since they were caught cutting down trees on Channing Way and throwing beer bottles out their windows.

Even worse, five blitzed Fijis went over to the Alpha Phi house to deliver invites to their annual Islander party. They got a little carried away in their presentation, overturned tables in the dining room, and did about $900 worth of damage.

I learned that my neighbor in the dorm, Brick, would be joining and also a member of Cal's football team, Dirk Albright, a solid six foot, four inch, 260 pounder who played on the line. The president of the Fijis, John T. McCarty (J.T.), nicknamed Dirk "Tiny."

For initiation, they locked all eight pledges in a room in their boarding house filled with cigar smoke. The windows had been nailed shut. In the center of the room were two cases of beer, along with paper and writing materials. We were told we had to finish the beer (and cigars) and write a play that we would perform that night in the Greek Theatre at the edge of campus.

The smoke was overpowering, and fortunately, one of our stronger pledges was able to get one or two of the windows open a few inches. Clark Bishop, nicknamed "Chip," the son of a golf enthusiast, turned out to be a wordsmith, so he took charge of composing a very clever, rhyming screed with parts for all. When inebriation and creativity had fully flowered, they let us out of the room, and we made our way up to

CHAPTER TWELVE — NEW ROOMMATE, NEW DIRECTIONS

the Hearst Greek Theatre, built in 1903 with money from Citizen Hearst in a style evoking the ancient Greek theater at Epidaurus. On the way up to the theater, Brick ran into the middle of Durant Avenue and was stopping traffic, while Tiny rushed out to rein him in and restore order.

There wasn't any security around the theater, and we somehow managed to let ourselves in, and the active members set up spotlights pointing up at the stage. It was a dramatic setting, with dense shrubbery and tall eucalyptus trees lining the periphery.

We delivered our lines in a mangled fashion, cavorting on the broad stage as first class bumbling buffoons, but enjoying every minute in the haunting venue.

* * * * * * *

There were two girls from Modesto living in Cheney Hall. Both seemed to have an unusual chemistry with me, and we hit it off in spectacular fashion whenever we ran into each other. I was more attracted to Mary, the taller of the two, than to Martha, a short young Mexican woman.

One night, I took them both back to my room around midnight. Jerry was already asleep, or so it seemed, and we crept in quietly without turning on any lights. Since the big glass window that ran across the length of the room faced the quad, there was enough ambient light to see plenty.

They tied me to the bed, and we engaged in a relatively innocent frolic. At some point, I had the distinct impression that Jerry was actually awake and taking in the whole affair.

My suspicion turned out to be correct because the next morning he could not stop joking about the escapade and later gave me a certificate he made that read:

> *Presented to:*
> *Mark "Whips & Chains" Ellis*
> *The Deutsch Hall freshman*
> *Whose sexual exploits*
> *Have most shocked and amazed his classmates*
> *in the dorms*

After this dubious honor, I got some great news. My former girlfriend, Laura, was accepted to Berkeley and would be attending in the fall. I suspected it was not a coincidence that she wanted to follow me here, even as she denied it. But I didn't mind a bit and looked forward to renewing our romance in the summer.

On May 17th, I was studying at the law library, the closest and quietest library near the Fiji house. I overheard some people talking about a big shoot-out in L.A. and that the head of the Symbionese Liberation Army, Cinque, had been killed.

It seems that 400 LAPD officers surrounded a house in South Central L.A., based on a tip they received about some heavily armed people inside. It was one of the largest shootouts in U.S. history with over 9,000 rounds exchanged between police and the SLA. The LAPD had AR-15 and AR-180 rifles, while the SLA had converted M-1s to fully automatic. They also had makeshift grenades they made using 35 mm film canisters. Police fired dozens of tear-gas grenades into the house, which eventually sparked a horrific conflagration.

When the shooting stopped and the fire had run its deadly course, the SLA dead included their revolutionaries known as Fahizah, General Gelina, Gabi, Cujo, Mizmoon, Zoya, and their leader, Cinque. Most of their bodies were found in a crawl space under the house, where they apparently retreated in the hope of escaping the intense heat.

Due to advances in broadcast news, the event was one of the first of its kind to be shown live, so Patty Hearst, along with William and Emily Harris, watched the entire violent siege on a TV in a hotel room in Anaheim, along with millions of other people.

CHAPTER TWELVE

NEW ROOMMATE, NEW DIRECTIONS

I left the law library as the sun was setting and was shocked to see red spray paint on the steps leading up to the library. Still wet, it resembled blood glistening in the after glow of a spectacular sunset over the Golden Gate. Someone who sympathized with the SLA had written:

Long live Cinque! Long live the SLA!

* * * * * * *

CHAPTER THIRTEEN

SUMMER OF '74

After finals, I made it home just in time to attend Laura's high school Grad Nite at Disneyland. I wore a tan canvas sport coat over a gold, pineapple-patterned Hawaiian shirt and flared pants. I was never one to pull an all-nighter for the sake of studies or inebriated excess, so staying at Disneyland into the wee hours with graduating high school students densely packed into Frontierland was less than appealing, but being with Laura made it all worth it.

The Disney people were masters at finding a million and one ways to merchandise a mouse, but there was an even more sinister side when it came to their security, which had authoritarian overtones. There seemed to be cameras watching your movements all the time, so if you tried to stand up on a ride, the voice of big brother came out of the darkness commanding you to sit down. And don't even think about opening a can of beer inside your car in the parking lot. The Disney SS would swoop in so fast it would make your head spin.

How could they see what you're doing inside your car? I wondered.

At the end of the night, Laura and I drove to Secret Cove, a beach on Portuguese Bend that could only be accessed by a narrow, somewhat steep, partially overgrown footpath. The intrepid hiker was rewarded at the end of the path by an idyllic beach and small, protected cove that happened to be favored by nudists.

Laura and I made love on the sand and fell asleep on our beach towels, with the sound of the gently crashing waves lulling us into a deep sleep. Several hours later, we awakened to the sun cresting over the bluff, its rays now falling on our naked bodies laying side by side on the beach. After endless hours studying for finals, I felt like I had won Monty Hall's vacation prize hidden behind Door Number 3 on *Let's Make a Deal*.

If it was not the beach, the next best place to be in the summer was the High Sierras. I went backpacking for the first time with my dad when I was about 12 and didn't really like it. I pooped out about two-thirds of the way up the trail, and Dad, unbelievably, carried my pack along with his own until we reached our campsite.

We went the next summer with one of Dad's friends, Dick Houston, his son, and another kid. I was a little stronger and began to warm up to the whole experience. We caught boatloads of trout using Super Dupers and cooked them up right away over an open fire. We drank the best-tasting water imaginable directly from the streams and lakes. One of the best parts was sleeping under the stars at an elevation of about 10,000 feet. I never knew there were so many stars and was overcome by awe and wonder looking at the vast Milky Way, via lactea, our spiral-shaped galaxy containing at least a trillion stars.

Since I am a Virgo, it was enthralling to watch a shooting star race across the Virgo Supercluster. The shooting stars were going off every other minute in a spectacular fashion. It was hard to get my mind around the immensity of the cosmos, filling much more than my peripheral vision could take in, with some 200 billion to two trillion galaxies somewhere out there in the great beyond.

It gave new meaning to the sage's words, "The light shines in the darkness, but the darkness has not understood it." Suddenly, I had a great appreciation for how small I was in the face of the infinite, and man's

CHAPTER THIRTEEN

affairs suddenly seemed somewhat insignificant next to the eternal.

Toward the end of the summer of '74, I went backpacking to the Hilton Lakes near Mammoth Mountain with my former roommate Jack, my neighbor Greg Jansen, and my old friend, Bobby Fawell.

Many of the tourists were gone, so we had the trail mostly to ourselves, but as we got close to our destination, we ran into two other backpackers headed toward the same lake. We stopped on the trail and talked to the men, one of whom had a military-style flattop, coke-bottle wireless rim glasses, and a large gleaming axe sticking up prominently from the top of his pack. Something didn't seem quite right about the two.

Later that night, we smoked marijuana around the campfire, and we could hear an occasional sound coming from the two men on the other side of the small lake. It was pitch black, of course, with the exception of the glow of our fire that lit up the surrounding trees. Someone began to joke about the "weird Harold" we saw with the axe, a reference to the character in Bill Cosby's *Junkyard Gang*. *The Weird Harold Special* had aired a couple months before our trip, so the tall, beady-eyed, clumsy character was fresh in our minds.

The more we smoked and the more we talked about Weird Harold and his axe, the more we freaked ourselves out. Frightened to death, none of us wanted to sleep alone in his own tube tent. Incredibly, all four of us slept in a single tube tent designed for one person. The next morning, we felt a bit sheepish about the whole matter and moved on to another campsite.

* * * * * * *

CHAPTER FOURTEEN

RECLAIMING THE HOUSE

I drove back to Berkeley in the tan VW Squareback. We were moving into the Fiji house at the top of Channing Circle, a three-story brick, Mediterranean villa with Italianate features built in 1928. Fortunately, when the guys in 1968 were forced out, the fraternity maintained ownership and rented its rooms boarding-house style. The old Fijis, mostly jocks, had nicknamed the place the "Brick Whorehouse."

In the front there was a broad, spacious patio perched above the street with views of the surrounding sororities and fraternities. From a wood deck constructed on the roof, there were magnificent views of sunsets over the Golden Gate.

The interior had handsome, hand-painted, dark wood beams running across a ceiling about 14-feet high, a broad sweeping staircase to the second floor, antique Asian rugs that covered the hardwood floors, a massive wood table in the dining room that looked like something out of King Arthur's court, and at the end of the table stood the fraternity's prize: a stained-glass window nine-feet tall created in 1912 to honor the memory of author Frank Norris, a member of the fraternity in the late 1800s.

Norris wrote novels attacking corporate monopolies during the

Progressive Era, such as *The Octopus*, about conflict between the Pacific and Southwest Railroad and ranchers in Southern California.

While Norris may have scored points with progressives at an earlier time, by the time I got to Berkeley, he was already being attacked for racism and anti-Semitic depictions in his books. Norris had studied under Berkeley prof, Joseph LeConte, who adopted a form of scientific racism and social Darwinism that fed the eugenics movement and, later, Hitler's gang of thugs.

Some thought Norris and Jack London were at the forefront of reforming the American identity as "a biological category of Anglo-Saxon masculinity," with his "exaggeratedly muscular novels."

In the large foyer of the house sat the so-called Norris bench, which included a very prominently carved inscription taken from *The Octopus*: "*Evil is short lived. Never judge of the whole round of life by the mere segment you can see. The whole is, in the end, perfect.*" With so much injustice, violence, and suffering in the world, it was hard to wrap my mind around this quotation.

We arrived a couple of days early to clean up the house, wiping down wood-paneled walls, cleaning the windows, the kitchen stove, waxing the floors. When it was finished, it looked more like a sorority than the typical frat house, which usually had the scent and appearance of my oldest pair of Converse sneakers.

They had a drawing for rooms based on seniority, and I was stoked to get my own room at the top of the stairs, across the hall from the president's room. It was about 10 by 14, with one window that looked out on a fire escape and a neighboring building. It had hardwood floors that were in rough shape, so I rented an electric sander and spent the next day or two on my hands and knees until I exposed the bare wood. Then I put a clear varnish on it. I found an old wood paddle in the subterranean garage that looked like it came off a whaler's ship and hung it from the ceiling. Then I bought a houseplant to hang off the paddle, and had my surfboard in the corner. I also found an old lifesaver that said "New Sea Wolf" "Emeryville," undoubtedly stolen from a restaurant by a drunken member of the frat, and hung it on the wall. At the end near the door, I had my stereo on a small table with a box of records on the floor.

The national fraternity made a big to-do about the return of the Fijis to Berkeley and held a banquet to celebrate the occasion. We all dressed up in tuxedoes. Jens from Salinas, who made a point of never wearing shoes to school, went barefoot to the banquet in his tux. Jens had a muscular build, a manly beard, and loved to listen to Moody Blues albums late into the evening. He was like a figure that had stepped out of the pages of a Steinbeck novel, somehow caught in a time warp.

The night before the auspicious event, a prostitute visited the house late in the evening on some sort of package deal that provided oral sex to each man, but nothing more, in the privacy of one of the rooms. After many beers, the anticipation of the moment led to a rather hasty conclusion, and left me somewhat dazed by the unsavory aspect of this rite of passage.

The banquet was held at the Claremont Hotel, a historic hotel about a mile from campus, nestled in the Oakland Hills. The property was originally developed by a man named Thornburgh during the California gold rush who erected a castle-like structure that burned during one of the area's wildfires. The charred site was later won in a game of checkers by Frank Havens and Borax Smith who formed an investment group to develop the hotel. Construction began in 1905 but met serious delays due to the San Francisco earthquake a year later, so it didn't open its doors until 1915. One of the best features of the stately white eminence was a unique fire escape that was actually a multi-story spiral slide that became a celebrated thrill ride for drunk teens and college students. Before the end of the evening, several of us had to sneak onto the slide and ride its twisting loop to the bottom.

The morning after the banquet, still hung over, we were taken to a hidden room accessed from the basement of the Fiji house, always kept under lock and key, known as the chapter room. As a secondary climax to the events celebrating the re-colonization, we were wrapped in white sheets (no hoods), blindfolded and led into the room in a train, with each man holding on to the shoulders of the man in front. As we were led in, it was quiet except for the rumbling whirr of an old fan. When the blindfolds were removed, it was strange to be in a place outfitted in 1928 with wooden pews built into the periphery of the pentagon-shaped room. Then a team from the national leadership of the frat took us through a ritual written in the 1800s, mouthing lines that included many high-minded ideals and Bible passages that sounded quaint and somewhat anachronistic, considering the freewheeling excesses of the previous days.

* * * * * * *

Mark crouching on skateboard in his room at the Fiji House

CHAPTER FIFTEEN

A BLONDE IN BERKELEY

One of the greatest things to happen to me was Laura's arrival at school. She went to live in the same dorm complex where I had lived, but she would come up to visit me at the Fiji house. She accused me at one point of only being interested in sex, and I had to admit to myself that was largely true. I was head-over-heels in love with her, and at that point in my life, it was difficult to separate the physical chemistry from the deeper qualities of personality and character that form more enduring unions. In my mind, she had all the qualities I would probably be seeking in a wife some day.

While Laura was an attractive blonde, she had never received the kind of attention she suddenly received in Berkeley. In Southern California, there were many gorgeous young women that resided along the coastal strip from Malibu to La Jolla Shores. Laura was one of many, but did not particularly stand out.

But in Berkeley, her intelligence and beauty were a rare commodity, and guys were suddenly paying attention to her and hitting on her like never before. When I went to visit her in the dorms, I met two of her new pals, Gary and Marshall. Both were Christians, which made me uneasy. Raised a Catholic, Laura was being drawn into a Christian group affiliated with Campus Crusade, which I didn't particularly like, and I became somewhat jealous and suspicious of her new male friends.

About this time, I got a letter from my old roommate, Jack, now at UCLA. He addressed the letter to Master Mark "No-Waves" Ellis, a dig at the fact that I was not doing any surfing in Berkeley while he enjoyed the waves easily accessed from Westwood. Also, the last time we had surfed together in Leucadia it was a large, hurricane-generated swell, and I was very tentative when the waves got over six feet. He was tearing it up, while I was mostly watching, which he chided me about unmercifully.

The letter, postmarked October 25th, 1974, said he delayed returning my letter so he would have a few more "bestial acts" to relate. "So you think you've become quite the fraternity man!" he taunted jovially. "Judging from your letter it seems you've finally managed to pull yourself together. How fortunate for all parties concerned. Seriously, it is great that all facets have joined together so smoothly—your frat, Laura, and no roommate, which is probably the best kind.

"I'll say that I now know what it is like to live with someone you are not as close to. It really makes me appreciate last year living with you, and I miss our fun. I am getting to know some really good chicks, which is reassuring, and I think it is going to be the sort of thing that is cumulative.

"So far this quarter, I've gone surfing four times. After a party at our house, I went to a frat brother's house in Huntington Beach. We surfed river jetty at about 7 a.m. when it was seven to nine feet and just smoking. I didn't even have a cord and was badly hung-over from wine coolers, but I got some hot rides.

"I was downstairs a few minutes ago in the TV room getting stoned and watching Johnny Carson. A girl called me up who was supposed to come over about 10:30 p.m. for a wine taste and a romp in my room, but she had to study for midterms and is going to the Cal game this weekend.

"I salute you as a gentleman and true scholar. Your commander in bliss, Homer the Slut. Some people call me the Space Cowboy ... Mark Ellis is the Gangster of Love ... I wish I could be in Berkeley; I've forgotten about communism and acne."

A couple of weeks later, Laura and I were in my room late at night listening to the new Eagles album, and she dropped the bomb that she wanted to break up. We made love together one more time. Then she dressed quietly and walked out the door. When I broke up with her at my high school graduation, I was very cavalier about it, and I know she took it very hard. But now, with the tables reversed, I was completely devastated emotionally.

For the next few days, when I walked to school past her dorm, my mind began to imagine her with other guys, and the little green monster of jealousy reared its head for the first time in my life, driving me insane. I had to change my route to school for my own mental stability and immerse myself in school and frat activities. Busyness was the only antidote to the pain I was feeling.

I penned a few lines of poetry as an outlet for my aching heart:

Patter
It rained fallen hopes
on Wednesday
Clouds burst my world
in two.
Sad dreams gave way
to misty sleep
no solace could be found
in the night.

A few days later, I wrote her a letter.

Dear Laura,

I have come to the painful conclusion that you were right in ending our relationship. The quality of my love for you had reached a state wholly incompatible with your new life and identity. It's safe to say it is all over.

The depth of my love could never be satisfied by chance meetings and idle phone calls. To be rejected by the one person who meant the most to me in my life broke my heart. I share your belief that it was probably wrong to be that emotionally involved with you. My emotions crept in slowly until it was all I could do to talk to you, laugh with you, hold you, feel the softness of your body, lie warm beside you, and be a part of you. I agree that it is best to put that behind me. I have examined the practical side, as you had, and now see that it will never work. Only my rational side can comfort me for this loss I feel. "Oh, love is gone, written on your spirit is this sad song."

Goodbye,
Mark

* * * * * * *

CHAPTER SIXTEEN

BUNNY FROM TEXAS

I usually studied at the library until about 11:30 p.m. Then I walked back to the house close to midnight. On one particular night when I returned, the house was abuzz with activity.

"What's going on around here?" I asked.

"Some woman from Texas showed up a few minutes ago, and she says she wants to strip in front of a group of men," Brick replied.

"Really?" It was hard to imagine, but I walked in the broad double entry doors, and there she was, standing in the foyer, talking to J.T. He suddenly bolted up to his room to get his stereo and proceeded to set it up near the massive dining room table.

"Bunny," as she called herself, was a little past her prime as a stripper, but that didn't matter one bit to a raucous group of college guys in the grip of testosterone overload. Most of them didn't have steady girlfriends, and the sexual revolution seemed to have bypassed the Greek system at Berkeley.

The slightly chunky Bunny hopped up on the table, and around 40 guys were filling every available chair in sight, starting to whoop and holler as J.T. put "My Girl" by the Temptations on the turntable, along with a succession of their greatest hits.

The Bunny had some undulating, practiced moves that seemed to confirm the representations of her professional past, to the delight of the guys slobbering on the edge of the table. Finally, one of the men couldn't handle himself any longer. It wasn't clear if she invited him or glanced in a knowing way in his direction, but Jason hopped up on the table, and she began to undress him. Soon, the two of them were splayed out on the same surface where we had eaten a few hours ago, writhing and contorting their bodies in a feverish display of lustful passion.

* * * * * * *

A couple of weeks later, I came home late on a Friday night after hitting some parties. Brick was in the foyer in rare form, having had too much to drink. He was a completely different person when he drank. He often bullied younger guys in the house when sober, but became a real terror when he had a six-pack in him. This night reminded me of my earliest experience with him in the dorms, when he was yelling out his window, but this belligerent monologue was like something hotly churning on a grease-spattered stove:

> *To begin with, we were drinking many beers.*
> *We were watching a commie pinko North Saigonese*
> *informational film about the Beatles.*
> *They were commies; they had long hair in 1962*
> *when we were learning to grow short hair.*
> *They must have been commies; they didn't even*
> *mention the Beach Boys.*

(Then he began to attack the first president of the reborn colony, J.T., who lived in the president's room, which had windows that looked down on the patio, directly above the front doors.)

J.T. lurks ... (he bellowed)
He was up there in candle glow light.
He's such a lurker.
He does it all the time.
You puppy.
Didn't I tell you sometime I would return to haunt you?
You think you're a sly son of a bitch
Because you locked your f_____ door,
I saw you in the window lurking
L-U-R-K ... got that (shouting)?
Lurking!
You lurked on me like I was a f_____ n_____.

We were hungry when we returned,
so Zeke got a whole box of salami, not baloney,
And he fried salami on the stove for 45 minutes,
We made sandwiches on the stove this thick,
He was going to blame it on Mrs. Allen (our cook)
for putting too much out at lunch.

You know who we met in the Phi Tau bar?
A f_____ from Modesto. He's a grape grower's son.
When he heard we were getting hassled, he grabbed a Colt 35.
He's living over there with a Colt 35.
His secret desire is to maim n _____.
The f_____ Phi Taus have a concrete bench that came out of
    Sproul Hall.
Zeke and I are gonna steal it.
What happened to Zeke?
He might have been caught pissing on the Gamma Phi's porch.

* * * * * * *

CHAPTER SEVENTEEN

THE PANTY RAID

Feeling a bit bored on a Saturday night, I caught word that Chip was organizing a panty raid. He and a small group were headed for Stern Hall, an all-women's dorm built in 1942 following a gift by some wealthy alums, Rosalie and Sigmund Stern. One of the noteworthy features of the place was a Diego Rivera mural in the main lounge, along with over 200 women rumored to be either over-sexed or under-sexed, depending on which Bowles man was telling the tale.

About eight or nine of us headed up toward the four-story, stately residence. On the way, one of the more inebriated in the group tore down a street sign and the arm granting egress from a parking lot. When we finally arrived at Stern, Chip discovered the front door was locked, so we went around to the back of his girlfriend's building and hoisted him up to a balcony on the second floor, where he found an open door.

Soon he was in, and we were standing around waiting for Chip to emerge with the purloined lingerie. Unbeknown to us, Stern had been the subject of several recent break-ins, and they were on high alert. While we were standing around, someone from their Residence Hall Association, known as a Hall Ass, called the campus police.

Within minutes, a squad car was coming up the winding driveway. As soon as we recognized the black and white markings, we ran across an expansive lawn and hid behind some tall eucalyptus, pine trees, and thick shrubbery. A policeman hopped out, whipped out his flashlight, and began a diligent search in our direction.

When his beam happened to fall on one of our guys hiding behind a tree, the Fiji in the headlights yelled out, "F___, let's go!" and we all began a mad dash through the woods that surrounded Stern, Bowles, and the Greek Theater. I was running behind Dirk Albright, the offensive tackle for Cal's football team. With Dirk blocking, I momentarily felt invincible, until we ran into a clearing and were shocked by the sight of six officers standing in a circle waiting for us.

I immediately stopped in my tracks and put up my hands in surrender, but Dirk dove into some dense bushes, and one of the officers jumped in after him. It sounded like two bears thrashing around in there until both emerged. Dirk's shirt had been ripped off in the wrestling match, and even the police were a bit wide-eyed at the sight of the brute lineman's chest huffing and puffing as he surrendered.

We were immediately handcuffed and thrown in the back of separate cars. We were taken to the campus police headquarters, where they proceeded to book us and question us at length. The interrogation took place in a relatively small office, completely dark except for one architectural-type desk lamp turned in my face. I was surprised because the questioning mainly revolved around the damaged street signs, rather than the panty raid. I denied any knowledge or involvement in the vandalism, and they sent me to a cell adjoining Dirk's.

Neither one of us felt much like sleeping, so we talked between the bars, with me doing my best imitation of Humphrey Bogart in the film *San Quentin*. "We're going to bust out of here, you see ..."

"Yeah, I've got your back," Dirk replied. The bantering went back and forth until they released us as the sun was beginning to rise over the Berkeley hills.

Soon we received a notice to appear before the Alameda County

CHAPTER SEVENTEEN — THE PANTY RAID

District Attorney, informing us we were being charged with resisting arrest. Dirk and I went to the meeting together, and Dirk made the astute choice to wear his letterman's jacket, which may have helped our cause. The conference was brief and convivial, and the D.A. seemed to want to talk more about Cal's football prospects. He explained that they routinely remove a certain percentage of lesser offenses to avoid clogging the system, and that our charges would be dropped. It was a huge relief and a lesson about the unforeseen consequences of seemingly innocent amusements.

* * * * * * *

CHAPTER EIGHTEEN

SEEING RAM DASS

In the previous summer at home in Rolling Hills, I had begun to listen to an underground FM radio DJ named Elliot Mintz, who seemed to be a close friend of John Lennon and Yoko Ono. There was something about his voice and delivery that was almost hypnotic, drawing in the listener in an intimate way with finely woven tales.

He began to talk a lot about a book called *Be Here Now* by Baba Ram Dass aka Dr. Richard Alpert, Ph.D., a former psychology professor at Harvard and colleague of Timothy Leary. The two were early experimenters with LSD at Harvard, discovering that using the drug seemed to open gateways to spiritual enlightenment.

After 500 acid trips, he was still seeking answers, so Alpert went to India and met the man that became his guru, Neem Karoli Baba, who renamed the young acolyte Baba Ram Dass. When he returned to the U.S., he turned a manuscript about his spiritual journey, with help from the Lama Foundation in Taos, into the bestselling book, *Be Here Now*.

Because I had turned away from traditional religion, I was open to the Eastern path promulgated by Ram Dass and rushed out to buy his book, which resonated with me and became my go-to guide for soul care. Thus, I was excited when I heard Ram Dass would be coming to the Berkeley campus to speak.

Some 1300 students, teachers, and others from the community packed into a stuffy Pauley Ballroom to hear Ram Dass, who requested all the windows be closed because drums could be heard beating outside in the plaza. When someone complained about the stale air, he said, "Stop breathing, and go into samadhi," with a sanguine smile. (Samadhi is the final enlightened state one reaches through meditation and the ultimate blissful union with the divine.)

It was a homogenously white audience, free of hecklers or political dissent (unusual for Berkeley), largely respectful devotees of Ram Dass and his message. George Harrison of the Beatles had already become an evangelist for Hinduism after he met Swami Vishnu-devananda in the Bahamas while they were filming *Help*. This led to several trips to India where he studied sitar under Ravi Shankar and met some influential gurus. Then he invited all the Beatles to travel there in 1968, and "the boys" studied meditation with Maharishi Mahesh Yogi. Because the Beatles were into it, a whole generation of young people in the U.S. were ready to cast off the tired traditions of their parents and embrace something new (which was actually older than Christianity).

There was a striking parallel between Harrison and Ram Dass. Each found the path of enlightenment through the use of psychedelic drugs. Harrison told journalist Mitch Glazer in 1977 that, "For me, it was like a flash. The first time I had acid, it just opened up something in my head that was inside of me, and I realized a lot of things. I didn't learn them because I already knew them, but that happened to be the key that opened the door to reveal them. From the moment I had that, I wanted to have it all the time, these thoughts about the yogis and the Himalayas, and Ravi's music."

As Ram Dass began to speak, one couldn't help but notice his Eastern attire and his Indian guru's portrait hanging above him. For at least three hours, he waxed on about the path of enlightenment, the Hindu Mother Goddess Kali, the Karmic cycle, and the benefits of meditation.

CHAPTER EIGHTEEN — SEEING RAM DASS

He led some songs and chants and finished with a Q & A that featured him asking and responding to questions he devised himself. *Was it too risky to entertain questions from the audience?* I wondered.

Afterward, as I meandered outside into the dimly lit plaza and trudged home, I felt enlivened by the evening, wondering if there was any way to integrate all the world's religions into one cohesive whole, something that seemed worthy of more exploration.

* * * * * * *

One of the games students played when signing up for their classes each quarter was to try and find at least one "mick," short for Mickey Mouse course, that would be relatively easy compared to the bulk of their class load. In the previous quarter, I had taken a class on wilderness survival taught by a Native American.

In the spring of 1975, I signed up for Medical Physics 11, which sounds daunting, but was actually a course about drug use and abuse, taught by Dr. Hardin B. Jones, a professor of medical physics and physiology. Jones had become troubled by the rising use of hallucinogens by Berkeley students in the 1960s and the potential impact on the mind, which led to extensive research and his book, *Sensual Drugs: Deprivation and Rehabilitation of the Mind*, written with his wife, Helen. He also became known for his outspoken opposition to marijuana use.

Dr. Jones was about as square and out-of-touch as a professor could be, with his bald head, baggy gray rumpled suits (probably in his closet since the 50s), and his warnings about the use of marijuana, which caused many students to snicker.

But one salient point stuck with me: that an ounce of alcohol is typically filtered out of the body within an hour, but THC, the psychoactive agent in marijuana, is stored in the fatty tissue of the body (especially the brain) for months at a time. The cumulative effect of this long-term storage in the brain led to the phenomenon known as pot-headedness, the professor maintained.

I knew a few potheads in high school and college, people who had become so mellow that they lost their edge, their drive toward self-improvement or advancement in conventional terms. While many of the students laughed and dismissed Dr. Jones, some of his warnings stayed with me, and I began to temper some of my pot use. The horror stories about people who had bad acid trips also kept me from following the hallucinogenic path of enlightenment blazed by Ram Dass and Harrison.

* * * * * * *

Mark at the Fiji Islander

CHAPTER NINETEEN

ISLANDER PARTY

The Islander party was the most prominent social event of the year for the Fijis, and bringing it back to the house on Channing Circle was a big deal for us. Guys spent weeks on the preparations, transforming the brick and mortar façade into a tropical Polynesian paradise.

An entire dump truck load of sand was dropped in front of the house, and guys with shovels and wheel barrows had to haul it up on the front deck to create a white sand beach. An entry hut with a thatched roof was constructed from bamboo tied together with rope. The primitive hut, accessed by a ladder, led to a swaying bridge over a newly created pond.

A couple of guys in the house with a truck followed the city of Berkeley's tree trimmers to snatch freshly trimmed palm fronds, which were used to cover the bricks up to about eight feet high along the base of the house. Coconut half-shells with leather straps affixed were designed to hang from the neck to sip Mai Tais or other exotic concoctions.

The party was usually held in May when the weather had warmed, so guys or gals could wear grass skirts, Hawaiian shirts, bikini tops, or nothing on top (guys). The Fijis got very creative about inviting their dates by presenting the coconut shells with the date's name hand-painted, along with a primitive invitation that looked like it was crafted on a desert island.

I invited Shelby Swank to the Islander, a dark-haired beauty from Marin County with sophisticated tastes and intellectual pretenses that made her somewhat aloof. We liked each other's outer facades, but couldn't really relate beyond that. She liked the image of who she imagined me to be, but not who I really was, which eventually led to a frustrating relationship. At the end of the evening, we went up to my room. I started to put a Beach Boys album on my stereo, and she immediately reacted negatively: "Oh, that's so passé." So I quickly changed to a new album by Traffic. We did some kissing, and I gave her a back rub. After all the build-up and preparation, the evening ended in a less than spectacular fashion.

A couple of weeks later, I was swimming at Harmon pool and ran into a guy from the Zete house named Ryer Pickering, an architectural student who drove a BMW and had a cool, friendly vibe. Somehow we got on the subject of becoming a ski bum.

"If you were going to take time off from school and be a ski bum, where would you go?" I asked.

As a Southern Californian, I usually went to Mammoth or June Mountain, the most accessible for L.A. people. Most of the guys I met at school, however, all went to Lake Tahoe, which was only a couple of hours away.

"If I was going to do that, I wouldn't go to Mammoth," he ventured. "That's just more of L.A. on the slopes. And Tahoe is all the Bay Area people."

"Where would you go, then?"

"I would go to a place like Aspen ... now that's a really clean ski scene," he said with a certain air of authority.

"I think I'm doing that ..." I said, without fully comprehending what I was saying, but the wish became the father of a snap decision made as I lolled in the sun by the pool in the blue speedo supplied by Cal's athletic department.

* * * * * * *

CHAPTER TWENTY

SUMMER ROAD TRIP

After finals ended, I motored south on the newly constructed Highway 5, which initially had warnings about running out of gas because there was nothing for miles between stops. I gave Laura a ride home at her request, which was a bit torturous because the wounds of our breakup had not completely healed, and I still had feelings for her.

When I arrived home, I had a talk with Mom and Dad, floating the idea of taking a year off from school. I was surprised that they were open to the plan, as long as I made a firm commitment to return to college when the year had finished.

I heard about a friend of a friend who had worked in Aspen during the previous winter, so I called her. She said she was planning a trip to Aspen in late July, and if I went along, she would introduce me to her former boss, and I could perhaps line up a job.

I quickly agreed to the idea, so I hitched a ride with Carla, camping along the way. I had gotten into skateboarding, so during some of the long deserted sections of highway in Utah, I would get out of the car and skateboard down descending stretches, with Carla's van following me. We camped one night near St. George, and as we got close to Aspen,

Carla started to go wild with excitement, insisting on putting John Denver on her cassette player singing "Rocky Mountain High" as we rolled into town.

We camped inside a teepee we found in a wilderness area adjoining Aspen. At this point, Carla and I had developed a road trip crush and had a romantic interlude inside the teepee.

Carla introduced me to the owner of the Mountain Chalet, Ralph Melville, a short stocky man with bushy eyebrows and a toothy grin. We seemed to hit it off, and he offered me an entry-level job as dishwasher in the kitchen and operating the snow blowing equipment to clear the sidewalks around the hotel. He asked me to start the week before Thanksgiving.

During the rest of the summer, I taught tennis on our backyard court, got odd painting jobs, worked briefly at a car wash and a paint store. While my parents were affluent, they insisted I work and earn money for school and my own spending. I had never received an allowance since I started working at about age 14.

In the last two weeks of August, we went to the La Jolla Beach and Tennis Club for the second year in a row of what would become an annual tradition. Built in the 1920s by the Kellogg family, the two-story unpretentious hacienda-style resort on La Jolla Shores had everything I loved: surfing in the morning, great tennis after breakfast, a pitch and putt three-par golf course, or laying on the beach in the afternoon. Then at dusk, we fired up the barbecue to cook fresh fish bought in the morning from one of the boats that came into San Diego Harbor. Blue-blooded families from L.A. and Pasadena seemed to book the same week every year, so friendships and business connections were cultivated along the shore.

Dad invited his friend from UCLA, Bob Perry, to come over and play tennis with us. Perry was the number one player on UCLA's team and went on to win the 1956 French Open in doubles with his partner, Don Candy, defeating Ashley Cooper and Lew Hoad in straight sets. He also made it four rounds at Wimbledon, so he was no slouch. Perry resembled

CHAPTER TWENTY — SUMMER ROAD TRIP

the actor James Stewart a bit, and having him in tow gave us instant court cred, allowing us to invite another great player as a fill-in for doubles with us.

To celebrate my birthday, I invited four friends to drive up to Westwood to see a reprise of *2001: A Space Odyssey*, Stanley Kubrick's masterpiece that first captured my imagination and wonder as a 13-year-old. I drove the VW Squareback with three other guys: my former roommate Jack; Greg Jansen, my neighbor in Rolling Hills; and my childhood friend, Bobby Fawell.

We were smoking dope all the way up the freeway, so when we arrived in Westwood, we were pretty high. I was trying to find the theater and realized I had to make a U-turn at one intersection. Unfortunately, it was illegal to make a U-turn there, and a police car was sitting nearby watching my boneheaded maneuver.

His siren came on, and we pulled into the side area of a gas station and began to panic. Marijuana smoke filled the car, and our clothes reeked of it. One of the guys in the back seat quickly stuffed our remaining weed underneath the back seat in a void that allowed that seat to fold down to create extra storage space.

One of the police officers came over to my window and asked us to get out of the vehicle. We stood there waiting while they searched the car and ran our drivers' licenses. It seemed like an interminable amount of time, and as we waited, the possible threat to our future lives and careers from a drug conviction rattled through our THC-riddled minds.

"Where are you guys headed today?" the officer asked.

"We came up here to see a movie," I replied.

"After searching the car, we found enough marijuana in the ashtray to arrest you," he said sternly and matter-of-factly.

My heart sank. They had us dead to rights. However, they didn't seem to find the stash we hid under the back seat.

"Since this is a first offense," he continued, "I'm going to write you up for the illegal U-turn." He handed me the ticket, and the police car rolled away. We parked nearby and actually made it on time for the epic movie, which became an even more spacey trip after our brush with the law.

I couldn't help but wonder if they would have arrested us if they had found the marijuana under the seat. I'm sure the officers sized us up as white punks on dope from an affluent area and decent homes. If we had grown up on the wrong side of the tracks or had different pigmentation in our skin, it might have been different.

* * * * * * *

CHAPTER TWENTY-ONE

A SOPHISTICATED MOUNTAIN TOWN

In taking a year-long intermission from school, I also wanted to take a break from drugs (other than alcohol), heeding the warning of Dr. Hardin Jones. I set out to see if there was anything to the idea of a "Rocky Mountain high." Was it real or just a catchy line in a song? My friends and I got stoned to do almost anything, even to watch a beautiful sunset. Perhaps the splendors of the mountains and trees were enough in themselves to get high, and I wanted to find out. The words of Thoreau resonated with me:

"I went to the woods because I wished to live deliberately, to front only the essential facts of life, and see if I could not learn what it had to teach, and not, when I came to die, discover that I had not lived. I did not wish to live what was not life, living is so dear; nor did I wish to practice resignation, unless it was quite necessary. I wanted to live deep and suck out all the marrow of life, to live so sturdily and Spartan-like as to put to rout all that was not life, to cut a broad swath and shave close, to drive life into a corner, and reduce it to its lowest terms …"

Aspen was a far cry from Walden Pond, but one could also argue that Aspen was the best place to be in the world in 1975, or so the sophisticates of the town seemed to think. I flew in to Grand Junction, then caught a ride with a recent transplant from Newport Beach who resembled John Wayne. He thought Newport had grown so much it was no longer the kind of place where people knew each other, but Aspen was still small enough for his tastes and to his liking.

The former silver-mining town seemed to revolve around the Aspen Ski Corp., the Aspen Institute of Humanistic Studies, and the Aspen Music Festival. Strolling down the streets on my summer trip, I was struck by the cacophony of music students practicing separately from each other in their rooms, the sounds wafting out of open windows, floating among the silvery aspen leaves, and I became entranced by the elevated atmosphere like a snake to its flute-playing charmer.

All three of the aforementioned institutions were the inspired brainchild of a Chicago businessman named Walter Paepcke, who happened to come out to Aspen to visit artist and architect Herbert Bayer. Bayer had just built a Bauhaus-inspired home on the outskirts of town. Paepcke and Bayer began to dream about creating a retreat for artists and thinkers in Aspen. Then Robert O. Anderson, the oilman that went on to found ARCO, visited the area on a hunting trip, met with Bayer and bought into their incubating vision.

Paepke's idea for the Aspen Institute was initially inspired by Mortimer Adler's Great Books program at the University of Chicago. The trio's first bash was a 20-day international celebration for the 200th birthday of German philosopher Goethe. Incredibly, the celebration attracted over 2,000 attendees, including luminaries like Albert Schweitzer, Thornton Wilder, and Arthur Rubinstein.

In 1970, gonzo journalist, Hunter S. Thompson, shook things up in town by running for county sheriff on the "Freak Power" ticket. An ardent slow-growth advocate, the position of sheriff seemed like an unlikely place for him to throw his hat in the ring to enact proposals such as decriminalizing all drugs, ripping up the streets and turning them into sod, and rejecting any construction that might obscure a view of the mountains. Thompson wanted to rename the town "Fat City" to dis-

CHAPTER TWENTY-ONE A SOPHISTICATED MOUNTAIN TOWN

courage developers, whom he termed "rapists" that should be dealt with as severely as any other criminal. He shaved his head for the race and referred to the Republican candidate, who wore a crew-cut, as "my long-haired opponent." Thompson was actually leading in pre-election polls until he penned a Rolling Stones article about the race that revealed the depths of his eccentricities and mobilized his opposition.

Even though he lost, his slow growth policies were embraced by many, which included banning Neon signs and eliminating billboards, which were mysteriously kneecapped under cover of darkness by chain-saw wielding residents. A four-lane highway through the center of town was rejected, along with hosting the 1976 Winter Olympics. A couple of high school girls led the charge to close off three downtown streets to vehicles and create a pedestrian-only mall. Car rentals were also banned at Aspen's small airport. Then a Land Use Code was passed that was about as restrictive as Sharia law.

After I arrived, I discovered that the owner of the Mountain Chalet, Ralph Melville, would put me up in a small A-frame cabin known as Heardle Cottage. As the only male occupant of the cottage, I was also to receive the only single room and eight female chambermaids would occupy the other rooms. I could barely restrain my glee! The room I moved into was covered with knotty pine paneling and had an old European ski poster on the wall emblazoned with the words: "Ski the Dolomites."

Ralph grew up in Braintree, Massachusetts, and was part of Dartmouth's ski team. He first saw Aspen in 1951 and fell in love with the place. A couple of years later, he bought two lots at the base of the ski mountain for $2000. He practically constructed the hotel by hand with another friend and by Christmas 1954, they had three of the first nine rooms constructed (sharing a single bath) and rented them for $2.75 a night. Eventually Ralph constructed 55 rooms and several apartments.

He met and married a ski bum from Pittsburgh, Marian Headley. Two weeks before their wedding, Ralph climbed 14,019-foot North Maroon Peak (part of the Maroon Bells). While uncommonly scenic, the face of the Bells is not granite, but mudstone, which is weak and easily fractures, giving the peaks the moniker of "The Deadly Bells" after eight people died climbing them in 1965.

Tragically, Ralph slipped and fell several hundred feet down the face, breaking his right leg, left arm, several vertebrae, ribs, and his jaw. He came to rest at the top of a cliff with his knee halfway up to his hip, and spent the night there in considerable pain while his climbing partner went to get help. He wasn't rescued until the next morning, but remarkably, limped down the aisle at his wedding.

As a result of that ordeal, Ralph founded Aspen Mountain Rescue, made up of volunteer mountain men who would drop everything to respond to emergencies such as this. He had also founded the Rotary, become a director of the bank, served on the school board, city council, and just about everything else in town.

Ralph and Marian and their six kids lived in an apartment upstairs at the Chalet. He was a model of the American spirit: sturdy, upright, and industrious, beloved in the community as a one-of-a-kind original. His work ethic caused him to begin his toils at daybreak and continue until darkness fell, often 80-hours per week.

Every morning, the hotel provided a complimentary full breakfast for 140 guests, so cleaning up their dishes was a chore. But before that, I had to make sure the sidewalks surrounding the hotel were free of snow and ice, which was real work. I reported at 7 a.m. and worked until about 11. Then I could go skiing the rest of the day. I skied back to the cabin at dusk, rustled up dinner, then went out to local watering holes like Little Nell's, the Paragon Ballroom, or the Hotel Jerome.

One day, Ralph pulled me aside with a grave expression on his face. His breakfast cook, a young, redheaded Michigander, had gotten into drugs, failed to report for work, and ran off, leaving Ralph in the lurch.

I expressed my surprise. "How could he do that? How could he let you down like that?" I asked.

"Well, I think the drugs were to blame. I've always believed in the Golden Rule," Ralph opined with his Boston accent. "Do unto others as you would have them do unto you."

CHAPTER TWENTY-ONE

I nodded in affirmation, even though I hadn't much thought about the Golden Rule. Ralph offered to train me to be the breakfast cook, and I leaped at the chance, anything to give up dishwashing and shoveling snow. The only catch was that I needed to start work at 5 a.m., a rigorous schedule if one wanted to stay out late with the party crowd.

So the next morning, Ralph began to train me to make coffee cake and cinnamon rolls from scratch, cook scrambled and fried eggs, bacon, sausage, and French toast or hotcakes on the big stovetop. I learned that if you heated the grill just right, after you poured the 16th pancake, the first one poured was ready to be flipped.

I got word from a friend at the Fiji House that Brick had been elected president of the house. How could a guy with such an unpredictable personality be elected president? He had been known to bully and harangue some of the younger guys, practically anyone who got under his skin. I talked to one of those unfortunates who was subjected to his bile, and they told me that if they opened the front door of the house and saw him, they would quickly shut the door, walk around to the rear entrance, and climb up the back stairs to their room just to avoid him.

The first two presidents, J.T. McCarty and Paul Workman, had been exemplary. J.T. was a legacy, solid as a rock, and his father had practically groomed him to be the key leader to revive the colony. Workman came from a strong Catholic family in Santa Monica and had solid values. One of his hot-button issues was racism, and if he detected it in any of the men, he would confront them face-to-face. He didn't have to dig very far because there was an undercurrent that ran through a few of the guys. They would casually and jokingly refer to blacks as "boons," which really caused Workman to erupt. This left a very strong impression on me because it wasn't easy to be that one guy to take a stand, so I admired his courage, even as I remained silent during such exchanges.

* * * * * * *

Mark with the girls of Heardle Cottage.

CHAPTER TWENTY-TWO

THE GIRLS OF HEARDLE COTTAGE

There was a colorful crew of young female ski bums working as chambermaids in the hotel that shared the cottage. Like me, they were often taking a break from college or recently graduated. There was Shona from L.A., who appeared to be in her late twenties, spoke with a soft, babykins voice, and resembled the movie star on Gilligan's Island.

Then there was Paula from Wisconsin, with pale white skin, fish eyes, large lips, and a strong upper Midwest accent. Jenny was very motherly toward me and called me "Pooh Bear" after the children's book character. I hit it off the most with Kristin from Ohio, an ex-swimmer who almost made the Olympic team, a fresh-faced blonde with a quick wit who always seemed to be ready for fun.

Most of the girls went home for Christmas, so I faced the lonely prospect of spending my first Christmas away from home. The week before Christmas, I made a rare phone call home and talked to Mom and Dad, told them I missed the family, and was sorry I wouldn't be with them.

The next day, Mom called back and said that she learned the Fleischman family would be in Aspen and wanted to invite me to Christmas dinner. I was over the moon with this news. They owned a condo on the slopes at Snowmass, a 10-minute bus trip down the road. I arrived at their place in the late afternoon on Christmas day. Erik's father, James Fleischman, a legendary New York businessman, had just come in from the slopes and was sitting on a couch near a sliding door with his skis just outside. He looked tan, rested, and relaxed, and his handsome face beamed a hearty hello as he extended his hand to greet me.

Mariette, a beautiful woman who had once been James' secretary, was busy in the kitchen. She was Catholic, and James was Christian Science; he did not believe in doctors. Somehow, they made things work, in spite of his commuting from California to New York in his private jet.

Their son, Erik, my drinking buddy, got into a fracas in the kitchen with his little sister over some infraction involving kitchen etiquette. Erik's older brother, John, always cerebral, always genial, understated, and wise, also attended Berkeley, and we got along well. To me, being with this prominent family for Christmas dinner was like entering a higher-level world. Yes, Dad was successful in his own right, but this family was on another plane. I could only compare what I felt to a vivid dream I had about being in the Kennedy family home in Hyannis Port in 1939 on the eve of World War II, when they were still untouched by tragedy, still pulsing with vigor, vitality, and infectious personal appeal.

The dinner conversation was polite and genteel, unlike my mother's family. When we got together for holiday dinners, you never knew what might happen, with boisterous verbal sparring or volcanic eruptions between my dockworker grandfather, Rod, and my sourpuss aunt, Shirley.

Erik invited me to ski with him and John the next day. Their skiing was also on another level. Between their Austrian genes, childhood lessons, and long skis, I could barely keep up. I was skiing on my dad's Head skis, 205 centimeters. Their skis were even longer, which seemed daunting when we got off into some thick, fresh snow, but somehow they sliced right through it with grace and ease.

Being with their family at Christmas helped ease the pain of family separation.

* * * * * * *

CHAPTER TWENTY-TWO — THE GIRLS OF HEARDLE COTTAGE

One of the maids named Shona came to me one day and confided that Kristin from Ohio liked me. Our personalities hit it off to be sure, but I had not really given much thought to romance because we lived and worked together. If we started dating and things didn't work out, it would be a disaster. Mona encouraged me to try to overcome my reservations.

Kristin became my first serious girlfriend since Laura, and our romance accelerated rapidly. One night, a group of us went to Little Nell's where they had a deal for a shot and a beer for a buck. I had two shots of whisky and two beers and was flying high, as were the other girls that worked with me. Included in our group were Steve and Louise from England, who worked behind the front desk at The Mountain Chalet.

We went back to the cottage and had more drinks. Someone came up with the brilliant idea to take the plastic serving trays from the hotel kitchen up the mountain and slide down in a big train in the dark. Each of us grabbed a tray and climbed up a ways on the mountain. Our drunken group then cast off together, each person sitting on a tray with their arms around the waist of the person in front, and we went sailing down the mountain, crashing at the bottom in a big ball of powdery joy.

Then Kristin suggested we sneak into the indoor swimming pool at the Continental Hotel. Kristin and I went over there by ourselves and discovered it was deserted at that late hour of the night. We went into the changing rooms and stripped down to our underwear, jumped in and began to frolic and cavort in the warm water. We were the only ones in the pool, but someone must have seen us and decided to teach us a lesson. When we got out of the pool, we discovered the changing rooms were locked with our clothes inside.

With a light snow falling, Kristin and I ran in the dark across two fields in our underwear to get back to Heardle cottage. When we blew through the front door everyone roared at the sight of our chicken skin shivering from the cold. Then Kristin and I dried off and hopped in the sack to warm up. The next morning when we woke up, Kristin sat up in bed. I was lying on my back, staring at her V-shaped back. With all her years of swimming, and missing the Olympics by only two-tenths of a second, her shoulders were larger than my own.

She got mad at me the night before when I started giggling during a romantic encounter. She thought I was laughing at her, which was not the case, but I remembered a line uttered by Randle McMurphy (Jack Nicholson) to Dr. Spivey (Dean Brooks) in *One Flew Over the Cuckoo's Nest*, which I had just seen:

"But Doc ... when you get that little red b_____ right up there in front of ya, I don't think it's crazy at all now, and I don't think you do either ... No man alive could resist that, and that's why I got into jail to begin with ..."

It was the first time I had particularly noticed this part of a woman's anatomy. I remembered Nicholson's line, and I started giggling, which Kristin did not find humorous at all.

On another night, one of the girls had some marijuana, and we all began smoking together. I had not smoked in a while and really had no desire, but I broke down and imbibed with a few puffs to avoid seeming like a spoilsport. They all wanted a "girls' night out" at the bars, but I was the fifth wheel.

"How about if we dress Mark up like a girl," Jenny teased.

"Yeah, then we can all go out as girls," Shona replied.

I wasn't having any part of it. "No ... no way," I protested.

Somehow, under duress and the influence of THC, I agreed to their silly plan, and they had a riotous time finding me the right clothes, wig, and make-up. I thought *Some Like it Hot* was hilarious with Tony Curtis and Jack Lemmon dressing in drag to escape gangsters, but this was perhaps the most embarrassing episode ushering in the decade of my twenties.

* * * * * * *

CHAPTER TWENTY-THREE

A SHOCKING DEATH

Sometimes, I helped Kristin and the other maids with their chores, particularly if beds had to be moved around to accommodate the needs of hotel guests. While they were working, they usually had a portable radio playing to help pass the time as they were cleaning bathrooms and changing beds. Mostly, the radio was tuned to Aspen's local station, KAJX, which covered the ski races in town.

The sports commentator who covered the races was a popular favorite in Aspen, Spider Sabich. He grew up near Lake Tahoe and was part of the U.S. Ski Team and the World Cup circuit, then competed in the 1968 Winter Olympics at Grenoble, France, when Jean-Claude Killy became a sensation by winning gold in all three Alpine events.

While Sabich could not beat Jean-Claude at the Olympics, two months after the games, he beat him in the slalom at a World Cup race and became the downhill champion the same year.

Handsome and charismatic, some think Sabich and Billy Kidd were the inspiration behind the 1969 film *Downhill Racer* that starred Robert Redford. Between his winnings and endorsements, he was able to move from a college pad in Boulder to a chalet he constructed in Aspen near

John Denver's house, costing $90,000. That was no small sum in 1971.

Two years later, Sabich was racing in the downhill against Jean-Claude and caught his arm in a gate at 50 miles an hour, flew up in the air and landed on his head. He suffered what football players would call a "stinger"—compression of the vertebrae—and could not stand. After being hospitalized, he slowly recovered, only to injure his knee twice during the 1974 season, which pushed him into retirement.

Sabich's fame in skiing circles was made complete when *GQ* put him on their cover with the title, "Pro Skiing's Richest Racer." Because of his injuries, he had to sit out the 1975 season, which led to his radio gig in Aspen covering ski races.

His live-in girlfriend was Claudine Longet, the singer and actress who had separated a few years earlier from husband Andy Williams, made famous for singing "Moon River," which my parents played endlessly in the early 1960s. The two met in Bear Valley, California, when Sabich came off the slopes, walked into a restaurant, and saw Longet sitting at a table with Clint Eastwood, Liza Minnelli and Robert Conrad. Sabich introduced himself, and an amorous affair soon began.

Because of Longet's marriage to Williams, she moved in some high-powered political and celebrity circles. She and Williams were very close to Bobby and Ethel Kennedy. When Kennedy won the California primary in 1968, the two couples were supposed to meet later that night. Kennedy even gave them a secret hand signal in his victory speech to alert the two of them as to when to leave their home in Bel-Air.

"It was almost midnight, and we were going to meet up at the Factory, which was a very trendy disco," Williams told *The Daily Telegraph* later. "Claudine and I were half-dressed and were lounging on the bed waiting for Bobby to make the little hand gesture that was the signal to leave for the Factory. He made it, then walked away from the podium, and we started to get dressed."

Williams got up from the bed to put on his tie when pandemonium broke out at the Ambassador Hotel. Robert Kennedy had been shot by a Palestinian with Jordanian citizenship—Sirhan Sirhan—who fired

CHAPTER TWENTY-THREE — A SHOCKING DEATH

multiple shots at RFK in the kitchen, one into his head and two into his back. Several other bystanders were also wounded.

Williams and Longet rushed to the hospital and joined Kennedy family members and other friends in an all-night vigil as doctors valiantly attempted to save Kennedy. "But it was hopeless," Williams lamented. "There was nothing that could be done. We went into his room and found Ethel asleep near his bed. He was already dead and was just lying there. What I remember is that everything seemed red. Red hair, red face, blood. Bobby was just this red thing on a bed. It was devastating to see him like that."

Astronaut John Glenn brought in a clean set of clothes to dress the senator's body. Glenn forgot or couldn't find a tie, so Williams removed his tie and Kennedy was buried in the singer's tie.

On March 21, 1976, I was helping Kristin in one of the rooms at the hotel, and the regular programming on KAJX was interrupted with a stunner: Spider Sabich had been shot to death by Longet! The popular, 31-year-old ski racer was dead at the hands of his lover. How could it be?

A week or so later, I went to the arraignment at the Pitkin County Courthouse, a stately two-story brick edifice from the silver mining era, and happened to arrive about the time Andy Williams and his family entourage arrived. I seated myself in the row behind the family.

When the diminutive Longet entered the court, she wore a simple dress with floral accents that gave her the look of a French peasant girl. She approached the judge with the meek, unassuming air of Joan of Arc.

People in town followed the trial closely. Longet claimed she asked Sabich to show her how to operate his gun, a .22 caliber knock-off of a German Luger, and it went off accidentally, with one bullet penetrating his stomach and pancreas just below the ribcage.

Longet's two young sons were outside sledding when the shot was fired. Her daughter, Noelle, aged 13, was the only other person in the home. She testified that she heard Sabich shout, "Claudine! Claudine!" and the next thing she knew her mother was dialing 911.

Local investigators made some dumb mistakes in their handling of the case. (Ironically, if Hunter S. Thompson had won his race for sheriff, he would have been deeply involved in the matter.) Without the proper warrants, they confiscated Longet's personal journal, which apparently contained explosive details about the status of the couple's deteriorating relationship. A blood test revealing the presence of alcohol and cocaine was also ruled out because it was conducted without due process. It seems that on the afternoon of the shooting, Longet had been drinking at a chic bar in Aspen.

After her arrest, Longet allegedly told a female officer, "I killed him," but this was also ruled inadmissible because her lawyer wasn't present. According to the testimony of two law officers, she told them she had pointed the gun at Sabich and said, "Bang! Bang!" before it went off.

The head of security at Starwood, the exclusive gated community where they lived, said he saw Longet twice on the day of the shooting, and that when the sheriff's lieutenant came through after the 911 call, he warned: "Watch it. This gal is a little ringy today."

Longet professed her innocence to Andy Williams and remarkably he bought her alibi and stuck with her for the duration of the trial, even procuring and paying for the best defense attorney money could buy. The defense ran circles around the prosecution and made them look like country bumpkins.

At the end of the day, Longet was found guilty of misdemeanor criminal negligence, received a small fine, and was sentenced to 30 days in the local jail. She was allowed to pick the weekend days she wanted to serve! I was outraged, and so was most of the town. It was my first sour taste of money and celebrity befouling the criminal justice system. It was as if Lady Justice had lost her way.

Ironically, above the steeply gabled entrance to the Pitkin County Courthouse is a six-foot statue of Lady Justice, made from pressed zinc to give off the appearance of silver. But unlike most such statues seen at courthouses throughout the U.S., this Lady has no blindfold. No one knows why it was never part of the original installation.

CHAPTER TWENTY-THREE — A SHOCKING DEATH

Some wag in the prosecutor's office came up with this rather demented limerick:

There once was a lady, Longet,
Who came to Aspen one day.
Along came a Spider
Who sat down beside her,
And she blew the poor bastard away.

* * * * * * *

Mark hiking near Aspen 1975

CHAPTER TWENTY-FOUR

SPRING SKIING WITH DR. DOG

Forty degrees in Southern California was uncommonly cold. But somehow, 40 degrees in Aspen felt downright warm and prompted people to ski in shorts or jettison their shirts on the broad sunny decks at the edge of the slopes.

On one bright and beautiful spring day, I caught the fever and skied in my Hawaiian swimming trunks and a very lightweight sweater. The only problem was falling on the hard-packed snow, which was very unforgiving on one's skin, leading to some bloody scrapes.

One day, I got on one of the longer chairlifts with a character who introduced himself as Dr. Dog. It was a warm sunny day, and Dr. Dog removed his shirt and sweater to reveal a muscular, tanned back and chest, covered with thick hair that resembled some sort of mangy canine. But then, overwhelmed by the pristine Alpine beauty, he began to howl as loud as he could from our chair. It wasn't hard to figure out how he got his nickname.

I learned his real name was Jonathan Elber and that he was in the real estate business in Honolulu. He also owned a banana plantation in a little valley near Hanalei Bay on the island of Kaui. "Why don't you come over when ski season ends," he suggested. "You could work at the plantation and surf your butt off."

"Oh, man, that sounds so good," I said. "I'm due for some warm water surfing. I'd like to talk to you more about it."

"Okay, meet me at the Hotel Jerome tonight, and we can talk further."

He skied off like a maniac, leaving me in the distance, but his invitation, if real, suddenly sounded exceedingly good to me as we neared the end of the season.

Kristin and I made our way to the hotel after dinner. Downstairs, they had a very happening bar scene and dance floor. We had been there a few times, and the DJ always seemed to play the Stones doing "Sympathy for the Devil" or "Jumpin' Jack Flash" at a certain point in the evening. We went out there, and Kristin went crazy when the Stones came on, working herself into a frenzy. In the midst of "Sympathy," I spotted Dr. Dog across the room.

I excused myself and made my way over to him. "Hey, I really want to take you up on your offer. Let me know what to do or where to go."

He went to the bartender and grabbed a bar tab and a pen and began to draw a crude map that showed how to get from the airport in Lihue, Kauai, to his banana plantation.

"Do I need to call you or make any further arrangements?" I asked.

"No, dude, just show up. Come ready to work, and bring your board. You'll have a great time."

After Easter, the streets in Aspen turn into a muddy mess, everything shuts down, and a lot of the locals take off for tropical climes. I knew it was time to leave, and I was ready, but it was hard to say goodbye to Kristin and the girls of Heardle cottage. We went to have a group photo taken at one of those places where you dress up in western garb. I was the lone cowboy in the shot surrounded by a bevy of scantily clad saloon girls, a fulfillment of every man's fantasy, including my own.

Leaving the mountains, I penned an ode to winter:

Perhaps you are not the one I met
beside Aspen glow and Winter's greeting.
And the soft traces that beckoned my spirit
have faded like seasons past.

I want to hear again your voice
whistling sharply between branches laden,
calling forth new fallen snows
that gently melt on silent faces.

But your last sweet murmuring
has passed unnoticed through empty boughs.
They all point heavenward, floating free,
and all your works like deep upon the ground.

* * * * * *

CHAPTER TWENTY-FIVE

HOME AGAIN, AND THEN OFF

I flew home to LAX, and Dad picked me up at the airport in his Jaguar. I had not driven much in six months and had not seen a crowded freeway. When he merged onto the 405 Freeway, I was scared to death by the speed and velocity of all the cars darting in and out of traffic.

It was good to arrive back home, but it felt strange because everyone else was still in school. My parents talked to me about getting my real estate license during my down time, partly because they were thinking about selling our house, and Mom had already made a special arrangement with the realtor, Marion Ruth, that I would earn a finder's fee if I obtained a license.

Inflation was soaring, and real estate investment and speculation was all the rage. My economics prof at Berkeley, Frank Levy, had provided me with the rather fundamental definition of inflation: too much demand chasing too few goods. With the feminist movement, tons of women had suddenly entered the workforce. Two income families could suddenly afford a bigger, more expensive house, fueling inflation.

The ranch-style house my parents paid $93,000 for in 1967 had dramatically risen in value to nearly $400,000. I really did not want them to sell it because I had already formed a sentimental attachment to the place I most considered home. Someone once referred to it as a mansion, which I thought was strange. It was a one-story ranch-style home with four bedrooms that was relatively modest. However, it sat on a lot that was a little over an acre, with a swimming pool and Jacuzzi next to the house, a tennis court they added, along with a barn for my sister's quarter horse, a former racer named Cleo.

I took a course from a company that provided practice real estate tests, and I memorized a lot of facts that I had no practical or experiential relation to, which made the study more difficult, but I was able to successfully pass the exam.

Kristin came to visit me, and she really hit it off with my parents and grandparents. My mind was in a place of seeking more travel adventures and returning to Berkeley in the fall, not a serious relationship leading to marriage. The passion was mostly one-sided, and she could feel it, which fed certain insecurities in her and an awkward postscript to our time in Aspen.

I decided I wanted to go to Hawaii, so I earned some extra money teaching tennis and a few other odd jobs until I had enough to book my flight and take off.

* * * * * * *

In early July, I flew to Lihue, Kauai, with a backpack, a surfboard, and directions to a banana plantation scrawled on the back of a bar tab. I rented a car, figuring I would follow Dr. Dog's route and find the place, then return the car when I had my bearings.

I set out from the airport following his precise instructions:

CHAPTER TWENTY-FIVE — HOME AGAIN, AND THEN OFF

> LIHUE TO HANALEI TO HIENA –
> UP POWER HOUSE ROAD (WAINIHA VALLEY)
> 1.5 MILES ON LEFT
> DOWN 100 YARDS TO STREAM
> ACROSS 1000 BANANA TREES.
> FRANK SPEAR, FOREMAN.

At the bottom, he wrote in cursive:

Frank,

Mark is my friend - he's willing to help 3-4 hours a day - please show him around.

Aloha,
Jonathan

How could I lose? I soon discovered this part of Kauai, the North Shore around Hanalei Bay, is rather wild and untamed. It's said the nearby mountains are one of the wettest places on earth, receiving some 600 inches of rain a year. So it was very lush, green, and tropical, but I soon got lost in the Wainiha Valley trying to find the plantation.

I pulled the car over into a ditch and set out on foot to see what I could find. I soon came across a short, squat, Asian man walking down the road who appeared to be in his 50s.

"Excuse me," I said. "I'm looking for Jonathan Elber's banana plantation. Do you know where it is?"

He looked me up and down and started laughing uproariously. "Oh, that Jonathan! He's such a bull-shitter," he guffawed.

My heart sank. "What do you mean?"

"It's no longer there. The guys he hired started growing marijuana instead of bananas, and the feds came in and burned everything to the ground. Some were arrested, and some ran off in the hills. You can hear them howling at night."

Reeling from the shock, I spent the night in my rental car, and the next morning, I drove back to Lihue. Completely dejected, I went into a McDonald's for breakfast. There happened to be a middle-aged man and his two young sons eating at a table near me, so I struck up a conversation.

We didn't get very far before discovering they had recently moved to Hawaii from Rolling Hills, California, my hometown. It seemed like a crazy coincidence.

"You can stay with us," the man offered. "I have to take care of some business, but call my wife and explain the situation, and she can pick you up and bring you to our house."

I called his wife on the phone. "Hello, Fran?"

"This is Mark Ellis. I just flew in from Rolling Hills ..."

She began gushing over the phone like I was her long lost son, and they invited me into their home for the next week. It turned out they were Mormons and wanted me to attend every function connected to their church. I didn't know much about Mormons. Their theology confused me, but I was impressed by their strong family orientation. They had something they called "family home evening" that included a lesson and some Bible readings led by the father. I had never seen my dad lead any kind of family devotions like this, so it left an imprint in my mind.

At the end of the week, they let me know it was time to leave, and I rented a room in one of the pole houses at Princeville, a short walk from the most idyllic beach I had ever seen in my life. I learned that the film *South Pacific* was shot at that beach and other spots in the vicinity.

I called home and told Mom and Dad what had happened. Mom said a friend's daughter was working at the Club Med Hanalei Plantation, a short walk down the road from where I was staying. I looked the girl up, and it seemed like she was in a drugged, trance-like state, which was probably no hindrance to life in paradise.

* * * * * * *

CHAPTER TWENTY-SIX
RETURN TO SCHOOL

When I returned to the Fiji House, it seemed very different. Most of the older guys, many that I admired, had moved out to apartments. Mostly, it was a whole new crew of guys, and I felt more mature after the year of travel.

One of the first people I ran into at one of the parties before classes began was Kim Schulz, the liquor company executive's daughter, who had been involved with my former roommate, Jack. She had never been interested in me romantically in the past, but suddenly, I picked up a different vibe. I probably looked different to her after the passage of time, and I had just returned from Hawaii, so my deep tan and bushy blonde hair might have been part of it.

We got sloshed at the party, then went back to my room at the Fiji house for a rather intense make-out session, but nothing more. The next morning, the encounter seemed to carry an air of unreality because we had always been friends in the past, and I always viewed her as Jack's girlfriend. She must have been struck by the same sentiment because I ran into her, and it was as if nothing had happened.

During the fall rush, Gary White, the Christian friend of my ex-girlfriend, joined our house. I was jealous of him two years ago because of his friendship with Laura, which I distrusted, but a lot of the guys liked him, and I began to warm up to his personality. He grew up in Piedmont, was built like a bowling ball, and played rugby and other intramural sports. It was a little weird to have a Christian in the midst of so many heathens, but he seemed to take the abundant cursing, coarse jokes, and taunting with good humor. Guys seemed to use the F-word in almost every other sentence, but Gary's voluble personality appeared to handle anything we threw at him. During the initiation, he was required to drink a case of Orange Crush, rather than beer, which seemed like it would put one at more risk of serious harm than alcohol.

One night, I went to a party at one of the other frat houses and began talking to an attractive young woman from the East Coast. I began to regale her with my ski bum tales from Aspen and casually mentioned the Spider Sabich murder.

"You know what really happened there," she said, lowering her voice.

"No, what do you mean?"

"Our family knows the Kennedy family, and the real story is that Claudine Longet came home and found Spider in the bedroom with her daughter. She went crazy and shot him ..."

I was so stunned I didn't know what to say. My red Solo cup, half-filled with beer, slipped out of my hand and splashed at our feet. Did she hear a story made up by Claudine that was transmitted to Ethel Kennedy in order to save face and create an alibi? Or, could this explain why Claudine got off with such an egregiously short sentence? Why would I trust a second-hand or third-hand account by a stranger at a party? Still, her story almost made more sense to me than the official version of events.

* * * * * * *

There was a two-story apartment building next door to the Fiji house and one of the rooms on the third floor of the Fiji house looked down into the rear window of the neighboring apartment on the second floor.

CHAPTER TWENTY-SIX　　　　　RETURN TO SCHOOL

The couple who rented the apartment did not have curtains, or at least never seemed to use them, and had sex with the lights on in full view of anyone who happened to be gazing in that direction.

When this was discovered, the room in the Fiji house quickly filled with at least 10 guys taking in the show, which confirmed Freud's observation that all men are voyeurs. The couple, about 25-30 years old, were slender and attractive, and their steamy sessions went on for a while.

One night, the guys in the room got overly boisterous, and Brick, our president, grabbed a glass and threw it through their window while they were in the heat of passion. The man happened to be a Vietnam War vet with a bad case of shell shock. None of us knew that any little thing might set off a reaction to the trauma he experienced in war, and this provocation happened to be frighteningly close to the ragged edge of his painful memories.

He charged out of the apartment and into the street in front of the Fiji house, yelling and screaming at the top of his lungs. We got a phone call the next day, and the couple demanded to meet with the president of the house, not knowing he was the actual perpetrator of the misdeed.

So Brick went over to their apartment the next day and sat down with them. It was incredibly awkward for all concerned, as the vet explained his emotional pain resulting from the war and the incredible invasion of their privacy, not to mention the glass shards all over their bedroom from the shattered window.

The woman looked very intently at Brick and said, "We think we know who did this."

"You do?" he replied. His eyes widened in surprise, and his body edged backward an inch or two in his chair.

"Yes, we think there is someone in your house that is mentally deranged. We've seen him hanging from the fire escape yelling 'dog penis'. "

Brick instantly recognized that she was referring to Zeke, who did some crazy things when he was drunk, like Brick himself, and that's why the two were such good friends.

"I don't have any idea who that might be," Brick replied, lying through his teeth, "but I can assure you nothing like this will ever happen again. And if we catch the person who did this, they will be disciplined by the fraternity."

* * * * * * *

There was a loose connection between Berkeley and Sacramento, with many friends and acquaintances of mine like Brick, Heather, Don, and others hailing from the state capital. In the summer and fall of 1976, unsettling news started to filter out of Sacramento about a string of rapes committed by someone they began to call the East (Sacramento) Area Rapist.

Ten attacks happened in the same neighborhood where my friends lived and created hysteria. At first, police tried to keep the matter quiet hoping to catch the attacker, but rumors were flying. So they held a town meeting, and 500 people showed up at an elementary school.

The rapist was reported to be a college-aged white male, six-feet tall, with a broad, muscular chest and hair long enough to hang out from a ski mask he wore. He seemed to watch his female victims until he knew they were alone and then went in between 11 p.m. and 6:45 a.m. through an unlocked door or window.

He used a knife, handgun, club, or stick to subdue the women and would sexually terrorize them repeatedly for as much as three hours, leaving them cut and beaten.

When the news got out, people began arming themselves and beefing up security at their homes. "The men seemed to be a little standoffish," a Mrs. Bradshaw told the *Sacramento Bee*. "Because rape has been swept under the cover for so long, our men don't know how to handle it when it started happening near us. They've always been told that no woman is really raped. But the women are scared out here, really scared. Everybody is paranoid. We are going to inform our men and hope they come out to the meetings and see the fear in the women. We are not going to be terrorized. We are going to get our men organized."

CHAPTER TWENTY-SIX — RETURN TO SCHOOL

Between the rapes in Sacramento and the rapes on the Berkeley campus, it seemed like the public awareness of the problem was bubbling up from beneath the surface of things, an unsavory stew that included carnal byproducts from the sexual revolution.

****

CHAPTER TWENTY-SEVEN

THE CAMPAIGN OF 1976

I never had much interest in politics, but when Jimmy Carter debated Gerald Ford, a bunch of guys crowded into one brother's room that had a small black and white TV and watched the debate.

Jimmy Carter's broad toothy grin and ingratiating southern style was off-putting to one of our new pledges, and he remarked, "He looks like he's whacking the mule!" to which I laughed, guessing at what the expression meant. A winning smile and telegenic presence had become of paramount importance in politics, ever since Kennedy debated Nixon on television, and people who watched on television thought Kennedy won the debate, and people who listened on the radio thought Nixon won.

When I ran into Kim Schultz, the subject of politics came up, and she made the comment that Kennedy was the best political leader in her lifetime. "He was so handsome," she remarked, which left me with the impression she was drawn to him primarily because of his looks. As a guy, I never thought about the idea of voting for someone because of their appearance, and the fact that Kennedy was "handsome" was not on my radar. But looking back to junior high and high school days, the people who seemed to win were usually the ones with the best looks and personality, no matter their platform.

Brick's term of office as president of the fraternity was coming to an end, and a sign-up sheet for the election had been posted on a bulletin board outside the bathroom. So far, the only sign-ups to run for president were two underclassmen, Brett Stevens and Carl Daniels. Both seemed like good men to me, but somewhat young.

When I was a sophomore, one of the older guys had suggested I run for president, and I was shocked, not thinking of myself as having any leadership qualities whatsoever. Public speaking made me nervous, and the one time I stood up within the august confines of the chapter room to say something, my voice started quavering.

Now that I was a couple years older, wiser (in my own eyes), and seeing that a domineering personality like Brick could serve in the position, I felt emboldened to present an alternative style. On a whim, I added my name to the list. I knew that on election night, each candidate would be called upon to give a short, five-minute speech at one of the chapter meetings, so I set about to prepare for that moment.

I went to the library and borrowed a book that contained every one of John F. Kennedy's speeches during the 1960 presidential campaign. In reading through the first 50 pages of the book, I soon discovered there was nauseating repetition in campaign speeches, but there were also turns of phrase and uplifting themes that inspired. Later, I learned that most of his speeches were written by his advisor, Ted Sorenson. It was also alleged that Sorenson was the actual author of Kennedy's bestseller, *Profiles in Courage*.

I found an album with Kennedy's speeches at a record store near campus and started listening carefully to his delivery and intonation. One of the younger guys in the house, Doug Cherner, popped into my room when I happened to have the Kennedy recording on, and I was attempting to mimic his voice. When he saw me and figured out what I might be doing, he started giggling. I sheepishly started laughing myself, realizing how ridiculous my bid to imitate JFK might appear.

CHAPTER TWENTY-SEVEN

THE CAMPAIGN OF 1976

The time rolled around for the election, held at one of our regularly scheduled meetings in the chapter room on a Monday night. About 40 guys crammed into the pentagon-shaped, dimly-lighted room. I knew I was the dark horse in the race because I had been absent for a year, and people knew less about me. Brett and Carl spoke first, winding their way through their short speeches about why they wanted to be president. It was clear they had not put as much time into their speeches.

Then it was my turn. I rose to my feet and began to speak confidently. I had committed my speech to memory, but clutched a copy of it in my hand, just in case.

"I have seen changes in this house that I would not have thought possible when I first set foot in the old Durant Fiji house in 1973," I began, with a serious tone. "This year we have seen money disappear, presumed stolen by one of our own brothers. We have seen an unprecedented amount of willful destruction take place. At times, our financial picture has been unpredictable and hazy. And at times, there has been a disregard for the rules that keep this house running smoothly and insure our survival.

"Let it be known that I am unwilling to witness or permit the slow undoing of those precepts upon which this house was founded. If we are in a period of drift, it can only be reconciled by embracing the firm foundation left by our forebears.

"The truth is this: there doesn't exist a more capable group of individuals than we have right here. In this room are the future leaders of business and commerce, law, and the arts and sciences. United, there is little we cannot do in a host of cooperative efforts. But the chain that binds us in a spirit of brotherhood is only as strong as its weakest link.

"In a short while, all of us will enter a world fraught with problems that will demand responsible leaders. But if we cannot be the keepers of this house; if we cannot be the masters of our own house; if we cannot guard, protect, and preserve it for the next generation that follows, we have failed miserably.

"So I say: Let this be the testing ground. And let us endeavor to build the strongest fraternity at Berkeley. It may not happen in a week or even a month, but let us begin."

There was a hush that had fallen over the room after I spoke, and I sensed that I had connected with them. The vote was held immediately, and I won in a landslide.

Brick stood up to speak, congratulating me on the victory. "I thought I was listening to JFK," he said. I couldn't help but smile inside, knowing his perception was less than a coincidence, but it felt good to have won something I could never have imagined, launching my ego into a new and higher orbit.

The next evening, I used the only pay phone in the house to call home to inform my parents. I rarely called home because it was a hassle to find the coins to call, and it wasn't really expected, unless there was an emergency. But they were ecstatic to learn I had been voted president. In the same call, Dad let me know he was completing the biggest real estate deal of his life, which involved the purchase of two high-rise apartment buildings in Santa Monica, known as Ocean Towers, for $17.0 million with the intent to convert the apartments to condos, from which he and his partners stood to make millions. The conversion of apartments was a controversial practice, and already political headwinds were beginning to build that would eventually outlaw their approach.

* * * * * * *

CHAPTER TWENTY-EIGHT

BOALT HALL GRAFFITI AND FALLEN WARRIORS

I studied at the law library, Boalt Hall, because it was a stone's throw from the Fiji House and was uncommonly quiet, if not a bit stuffy. However, their restrooms were not stuffy and featured a singular brand of political discourse scrawled on the metal walls inside the stalls that was not your garden-variety graffiti.

Several of these politically-oriented screeds featured a question or comment with numbered responses below to fill in using one's demented creativity.

Name your favorite racist (one began)
1. *Earl (the Pearl) Butz*
2. *Hirohito*
3. *Ian Smith*
4. *Adolph (Hitler or Coors?)*
5. *Ron Dellums*
6. *Archie Bunker*
7. *Cesar Chavez*
8. *Bob Dole*
9. *Hayakawa*

10. Stokely Carmichael
11. people submitting 5, 7, 10, 12, 13
12. Vida Blue
13. Israel
14. Amy Carter
15. Bugs Bunny

What will be Jimmy Carter's first act as president?
1. unnatural
2. pardon President Ford
3. declare the peanut the national fruit

If you can't get justice, get revenge.

Martha Mitchell will always be remembered as:
1. a beautiful woman
2. John's beloved wife
3. a passable _____
4. a headline grabbing _____
5. a _____ grabbing lesbian
6. Dick Nixon's spiteful mistress
7. who?
8. a twit
9. a busy signal
10. a bad lay
11. the small enchilada
12. long as she lives (d)
13. none of the above
14. some of the above
15. Bart Starr's pen pal
16. cheap throat
17. Arkansas's contribution to the world
18. the mouth that roared

CHAPTER TWENTY-EIGHT   BOALT HALL GRAFFITI AND FALLEN WARRIORS

We all got some very sad news that Cal's star quarterback, Joe Roth, passed away due to melanoma at 21-years-old. He set all kinds of records during the year I was absent, so I missed his final season, but I still felt the sense of tragedy of losing someone at the prime of life, whose promise was yet unfolding. Moved by the injustice and fragility of life, I sat down and penned a few words:

A mortal blow this night for Blue and Gold,
and many whose gaze he held.
The finest vision of youthful strength and courage.
No future seemed brighter, only greatness divined.
His cup was filled to overflowing.
A tragic twist of fate, then emptied by an unseen hand.
Amid dreams of glory, a pause,
and something vital slipped away.
He attested to a faith unshrinking
not accepting other's lamenting.
Walking to and from a campus he loved.
A heart strengthened with solace from above.
As church bells throb, countless students are weeping.
A fighter to the end, the dauntless Joe Roth.

* * * * * * *

CHAPTER TWENTY-NINE

GOVERNING

Overseeing a group of guys that are forced to study hard due to the competitive pressures, play hard on their time off (often involving excessive drinking), and sometimes skating on the thin edge of the law brought me a measure of sobriety. It seemed like the future of the fraternity hung by a slender thread, and if there weren't guardian angels hovering about, some tragic incident might happen at any moment as a result of the excesses with drinking and driving, or clambering about while inebriated on precarious perches like our fire escape.

The cabinet officers and I decided we needed to tighten things up a bit, so we started fining guys for all manner of sundry offenses, like being late for dinner. Some of the guys began to grumble and refer to us as Nazis. It was a classic confrontation between the more serious, studious guys and the party animals.

The wood-paneled living room of the house had a gigantic European-style fireplace that a person could almost walk into. So one night we built a roaring fire there, and I gathered the men to welcome our class of 15 new initiates. They were involved in a pledge program to train them as to their various chores and duties around the house, and they had just finished cleaning things up, so I was proud of their effort. The lights were out in the room, except for the fire. I stood next to the hearth and began to speak:

"A famous American once said, 'An ounce of loyalty is worth a pound of cleverness, especially if it means that cleverness is employed to shortchange your pledge brothers, the guys who are really doing a job around here.

"We don't care who performs their duties in the house as long as someone does. This implies self-sacrifice, it implies taking the initiative if need be. It means that if you step into the kitchen at 10:00 Sunday night, and it's a mess, you take the initiative to clean it up because no one else will.

"Remember, this is the training ground for creating those outstanding qualities necessary for success in life. The pledge program offers the best training in subordinating oneself for the welfare of the group—controlling your own appetites and desires for the sake of something greater than oneself.

"The whole experience isn't about you or me. It's about us. It's about being one. It's about brotherhood. If you succeed through the rest of the pledge program as you have tonight, we will all be one."

One of the perks of being president of the house was heightened status with certain sorority girls that might be impressed by such a thing. At one of our mixers with the Pi Phi house, I developed instant chemistry with a classy gal named Bev Scowcroft, and decided I would invite her to our Islander party.

Our biggest party of the year, the Islander, was as rollicking and free-wheeling as ever, with high-octane Fiji punch, kegs of beer flowing, and women dressed in scanty Polynesian attire. I invited Bev up to the president's room, the largest private room in the house, situated above the front entrance, with its own bath. Rock music was blaring outside, and inside my room, I began to kiss Bev passionately as we stood near the bed.

Undoubtedly, I had had too much to drink. I grabbed Bev and forcibly pushed her onto the bed. Her eyes widened with alarm, fearing I was about to force myself upon her. She pushed me away, rolled off the bed, and got to her feet.

"I have to go," she said, and made a hasty exit. The last thing on my mind was a forced sexual encounter, but the beer led to an uncharacteristic aggressiveness that triggered a frightful response in her.

I felt some remorse and embarrassment the next day, and my budding romance with Bev evaporated. Someone once said that the difference between socialism and communism is the difference between seduction and rape. I learned a painful lesson that seduction (and taking it slow) always produced better outcomes than overly aggressive advances.

* * * * * * *

CHAPTER THIRTY

THE SOCIOLOGY OF SPORTS

I n the fall of my senior year, I enrolled in the class, Sociology of Sport, taught by Professor Harry Edwards, the civil rights activist who organized the black power salute by Tommie Smith and John Carlos at the 1968 Olympics in Mexico City. An iconic photo on the cover of *Life* magazine showed the two athletes raising black-gloved fists in the air with their heads looking down on the medals platform, which created a controversy.

Tall and well built, Edwards had been a discus thrower on the San Jose State track team. He paced the floor of the lecture hall with a larger than life presence, holding forth on all manner of subjects, from racism in America to his own prowess in the bedroom: "When the lights go down and the shades are drawn, it's every man for himself," he cracked during one lecture.

He believed a disproportionate number of blacks pursued an illusory dream of making it in sports because that was perceived as their only path to achieve the American Dream. He saw painfully few role models drawing young blacks into the world of academic achievement, which he lamented.

My perception was that racism and anti-Semitism were declining in America, but others, apparently, felt otherwise. I did not hold the strident, hostile views of my grandfather and his generation, and I did not have any close friends who held those views, even if the discourse within the fraternity was disturbing.

An unfortunate series of incidents had begun to happen about that time involving the Chabad House, a traditional Jewish center that had opened a few years earlier in a location near us surrounded by fraternities and sororities.

A leaflet showed up at the Fiji House with this arresting headline: "Stop Campus Nazis." It charged that religious objects at the center were destroyed on two occasions by people from nearby fraternities.

"This is but the latest in a series of anti-Semitic, pro-Nazi actions on campus, generally emanating from the fraternities," it stated. "Last spring, a group of 20 people from the Skull & Keys drinking club, which apparently consists of the worst elements in all the fraternities, gathered in front of Chabad House, shouting 'Burn the Jews' and 'Hitler was right' as the fence was torn down. This took place on Adolph Hitler's birthday."

The screed, written by the "Committee Against Racism," went on to lament that the number of black U.C. students had declined from 3,000 in 1972 to 1,100 in 1977, partly blamed on the Bakke decision by the California Supreme Court in 1976. Allan Bakke, a 35-year-old white male, was rejected by a number of medical schools, and he sued the Regents of the University of California over racial quotas.

The California Court ordered Bakke admitted to UC Davis Medical School, and the school's policy of reserving 16 seats for minority students was struck down. Pending further review by the Supreme Court, the university could not take race into account in admissions.

The pamphlet linked the revival of interest in fraternities to a white backlash against affirmative action programs, which didn't correlate in my mind, but I couldn't deny the casual disparagement of blacks within my own fraternity. "Historically, racism in fraternities

CHAPTER THIRTY — THE SOCIOLOGY OF SPORTS

is well known and ranges from social segregation to more active forms. Fraternities that show any evidence of perpetuating the racism for which they are known have no place at a public university and should be abolished ... to fight back in an organized way, join the Committee Against Racism, meeting next Wed. 9PM Oxford Hall rm#2. Greg, Andy, and Adrian."

I got a call from the campus newspaper, the *Daily Cal*, wanting a quote about the anti-Semitic incidents directed against Chabad House. "I deplore any attacks on Chabad House," I was quoted as saying. "Our fraternity stands against anti-Semitism, and we will stand with the Jewish people in these assaults."

Later, I ran into Zeke, who happened to belong to Skull and Keys. "I read your quote in the newspaper. It sounded so political," he said, with a look of derision and disgust.

It was the first time I realized that being "political" was a pejorative term in some people's eyes. Having been mesmerized by the Kennedy charisma, I lost sight of the fact that Joe Six-pack saw things a little differently in the world.

* * * * * * *

One of the major parties of the year was the Black Diamond, which had a stylish ambiance to it, as compared to our Military Brawl party, in which the guys and their dates dressed in military fatigues and crawled through an obstacle course with the sounds of background machine gun fire to enter the party.

After the Diamond, I was up in my room with my date, and I heard the most horrendous sound of yelling and breaking glass. It seems that five young black men from neighboring Oakland entered the house and wanted something to drink.

"Haul ass!" Burt McTeague bellowed to the young men. "Get out of here now," he ordered. One of the young men approached McTeague in a menacing fashion, started to raise his fist, and McTeague popped him in the jaw, knocking him back on his heels. McTeague happened to be on Cal's boxing team, so he knew how to throw a punch, but pandemonium ensued. The other young blacks grabbed liquor bottles and began throwing them, as everyone took cover. The sound of the bottles shattering on the stone stairway was frightening.

I came down the stairs at the moment the young men took off running. Broken glass was everywhere, but no one had been injured in the melee, to my relief. Everyone gathered around McTeague, as he recounted his version of the events. It was a narrow brush with disaster.

* * * * * * *

CHAPTER THIRTY-ONE

CHAPTER REVOLT

As president of the house, I attended IFC meetings, which involved the heads of all the fraternities and sometimes, campus administrators. Because of public incidents involving excessive drinking, vandalism, and anti-Semitism, a stern warning was given about a possible crackdown coming from the university that would be severe.

I shared the unwelcome news with the cabinet, and we reluctantly decided it would be unwise to break into the grounds of the Greek Theater to stage our initiation rites. When I shared this news with the rest of the guys and that we would have to curtail some of our drunken revelry, I could feel the heat rising in the room.

Performing in the Greek had become a cherished tradition, and beer was the mother's milk of fraternal relations. Our cabinet already stood on shaky ground with our heavy-handed approach to fining guys for relatively minor offenses. Now a seditious spirit began to inflame many of the men.

A previous president of the house, Monty, posted a lengthy letter of protest on a bulletin board near the restroom.

"I feel compelled to write this open letter in light of what has taken place here in the last few days," he began. "Last night, I was struck by the reality that this fraternity has changed. I feel that many people will miss out on the good times that can be had only while in college. Because of the changes, people will be inhibited to do something a little out of line.

"This last quarter of scholarship was the worst we have ever had. At the same time, this was the quietest, least derelict quarter I've seen around Phi Gamma Delta. Personally, I've been able to do more than my share of being a derelict and still maintain a 3.4 GPA. In fact, if it were not for the likes of the derelicts, our GPA would be even lower. For the most part, the partiers in this house have better grades than the studiers. I think it's been proven that it's possible to be a good student and have a good derelict time at the same time.

"In the old days, we could get heated and derelict whenever we wanted, we got higher grades than we do now, we broke things but repaired them and kept the house in very good shape, we had great fun and felt a real sense of brotherhood, all of which is starting to disappear. If this is a result of these changes, it's my opinion something is wrong.

"I will have to abide by the decisions, regardless of how I feel about it, or suffer the consequences. If my actions cross the boundaries that have now been set up, then fine me.

"The Phi Gamma Delta I joined seemed to be much better than the Phi Gamma Delta I'm a member of now. Therefore I'm not going to change my attitude or act around this fraternity, at least until it's proven to me the new way is better. If the cabinet feels these actions are a violation, then fine me.

"To anybody who feels as I do, let me know when you're going to get heated, and I'll try to make it. If anyone wants to talk about the old days or anything concerning this, I'd be more than willing, and the first one's on me!"

I felt wounded by the open challenge to my leadership, especially coming from a previous president. But Monty was such a beloved figure in the house, I couldn't stay mad at him too long. I quietly removed his message and stuffed it under a pile of papers in my room.

CHAPTER THIRTY-ONE CHAPTER REVOLT

The week before initiation, I was presented a letter from the 10 pledges about to undergo their official induction, always a drunken affair in the past.

"We the undersigned realize that drinking plays a part during the initiation week and that this drinking done on my behalf is voluntary and not forced upon me. Thus, I cannot and will not hold the fraternity of Phi Gamma Delta or any officer thereof responsible. Signed: Bill, Carl, Craig, Stuart, Dick, Ned, George, and Matt."

When the day of the initiation arrived, I was met by an angry group that openly challenged the decision about the Greek Theater. Confronted by about 15 angry guys filled with beer and ropes handy, I backed down.

"This is just bullshit," one of the rebels shouted. "Those who want to maintain a great tradition can follow me."

"If you are determined to go to the Greek, I'm willing to look the other way," I said. Faced with a no-win, Pontius Pilate-like predicament, I said, "I'm washing my hands of this."

With animalistic shrieks and whoops, the men charged off to the Greek Theater, and I stayed home with a few others, licking my wounded pride, wallowing in self-pity over my failure in leadership.

* * * * * * *

CHAPTER THIRTY-TWO

SKULL & KEYS

A notice appeared on the Fiji bulletin board announcing the 87th running for Skull & Keys, with about 30 neophytes listed, including my name and one other member of our chapter, Chris Mason. It was a who's who list of those it considered campus leaders, party animals, and other notable guys on campus.

The esteemed (and somewhat controversial) novelist from our house, Frank Norris, helped found the organization in 1892, patterned after the Skull & Bones secret society at Yale. Like the Yale group, they met in a facility known as The Tomb. I was told that in their last initiation, each person had to drink a case of warm beer, do sit-ups in Channing Circle until they puked, followed by other drunken rites of passage.

They were more raucous and outrageous in their actions than any other group on campus. I might have been game in my freshman or sophomore year, but as a senior who already had a year of travel under my belt, I had no appetite for their shenanigans and declined the offer. The timing seemed ironic, considering what I had been dealing with at my own house.

Someone within the Fiji house had scrawled "MUST DIE" by my

name on the public invitation. It was unsettling, but I did not take it as a threat. It was simply a reflection of the recent angst.

I received a letter from the national fraternity sent to four presidents around the country requesting each to write an essay on the subject of the "New Morality," asking how standards of morality had changed in the last 20-50 years, and whether alcohol, drugs, and sex are problems in our houses. Since I had no fixed standard of ethics and morality for myself, it was a difficult subject for me to tackle with any authority or credibility, but I reluctantly accepted.

Another one of the presidents, Keith Barnaby (Colgate 78), wrote: "Awareness of the thoughts of others has had many beneficial side effects, such as the acceptance rather than repression of certain sects in our society formerly thought to be queer or sick."

Jay Matzke (Nebraska 79) noted: "Twenty years ago the average college student didn't know what an amphetamine or speed was. The only time marijuana was mentioned was when someone heard a drummer in a rock band could play faster while under its influence. And sex, what used to happen in a car now takes place in a dorm or fraternity room. So morality hasn't changed completely, but temptations have increased ... The New Morality is a more open and candid approach to ideas and problems that were once dealt with by whispers in dark secluded rooms."

James Lee (Minnesota 78) wrote: "We must be realistic and accept that fact that some individuals will prefer to smoke marijuana while others will prefer to drink beer. A liberal view on both sides is necessary to avoid a split. Yet the use of drugs within the chapter house cannot be tolerated, lest we give reason for being labeled a drug den ... The New Morality says if it feels good, do it. Free love and living together are no longer uncommon. The ideas are certainly not new; they've just quit making rumble seats ... The ultimate molding of a person's character is most influenced by his parents in his formative years."

Those words resonated with me, because I recognized a void within myself due to a lack of parental training in ethics and morality. Of course, I picked up cues about right and wrong by osmosis within the family.

But sadly, my ethical compass was loosely hashed together from dubious cultural influences on TV sitcoms or reading the Playboy Forum. My instincts told me there must be some enduring values, something solid, somewhere to be found, but I wasn't sure where to find it. Seeing Ram Dass and reading his book, *Be Here Now*, I felt was a start along this path of enlightenment. Perhaps a way could be found to unite the best elements of all the world religions.

For my contribution to the magazine, I wrote: "An era of amorality has mistakenly been labeled an era of new morality. Perhaps young people are never forced to examine and construct their own belief system. In the educational process, a student may never have to ask such ultimate questions as 'What's life about? What am I here for?' The conventional wisdom of my generation has been, 'You do your thing. I'll do my thing. And if we both meet somewhere in between, it's beautiful.'

"The use of drugs spans a broad spectrum between good, bad, and ugly. Any drug, including alcohol, used excessively can create problems for the individual. But it is when these excesses lead to destructive acts against the house, its members, or the individual's own health that a special duty of care arises. The group must exercise its power and influence to help that individual for, in many cases, he will not help himself."

****

CHAPTER THIRTY-THREE

WOODY'S PEP TALK

Don Decker, our house treasurer; Monty, our former president; and I were flown to Ohio State to attend a Fiji Leadership Academy. Monty had been nominated for the national fraternity's highest award, and he put together a slick, impressive campaign for himself that looked like it had been done by a professional marketing firm. He actually beat all the competition and won the award, a big honor for our fledgling reborn chapter in Berkeley, hidden in the brackish backwaters of the fraternity, which really was strongest in the South and upper Midwest.

One morning, about 30 or 40 of us were ushered into a room on the campus, and the football coach, Woody Hayes, had been invited to address our group with a motivational talk. He was a big, rangy guy with a strong jaw, broad Midwestern shoulders, and gray hair slicked back past a wide forehead. The coach looked like a heftier, meatpacking version of LBJ.

I was surprised when he began to talk about a little book titled *Word Power Made Easy*, which he said he gave to all his players. He challenged them (and us) to read the book and learn a new word every day. It was part of his vision of producing a scholar athlete.

"If I let you come here to college and you flunk out of school, I'm cheating you," he said. "Going through this silly little book helps enormously."

"The fact that I'm a football coach, it's a competitive thing. I despise for people to beat us. That's why when I get good football players, I'm not going to let someone else beat us because I'm cheating myself, and I'm cheating my players if we don't get the best out of 'em.

"You know, I might give you a little advice today. One thing you cannot afford ever to do is to feel sorry for yourself. You can't do it. You cannot feel sorry for yourself because that's what leads to drugs, what leads to alcohol, and those things that tear you apart.

"In football, we always say, 'That other team can't beat us. We have to make sure that we don't beat ourselves.' And that is what a person has to do, too—make sure that they don't beat themselves. It takes an awful big man to beat you. So many times, I have found people smarter than I was. I found them in football, bigger, they could run faster, could block harder, they were smarter people than I.

"But you know what they couldn't do? They couldn't outwork me. I ran into coaches that I coached against who had a much better background than I did, knew a lot more football than I did, but they couldn't work as long as I could. They couldn't stick in there as long as I could.

"I tell my players I don't want them on the football field if they show any signs of apathy. Apathy! *(He growled when he said the word.)* Avoid it like the plague! It's the damndest thing in the world, and you will run into these guys on the campus. They say, 'Why get up in the morning? Why play football? You work too hard; why do that? Come on and have a joint with me.'

"Hell, he'll sit and look at his shoe for an hour. And he's thinking great thoughts about what the hell he's going to do. You think I'm kidding? I know people as apathetic as hell, and they're going nowhere. There are a hell of a lot of apathetic people, and they take a lot of people with them. We all have a tendency to be lazy. I don't know if it's body chemistry or mind or a combination. It may be both. We all have a tendency to ease off at times. That's why you need good teachers and good

CHAPTER THIRTY-THREE — WOODY'S PEP TALK

coaches to push you a little bit. We all have to be pushed.

"If you only pick up one word today, learn to avoid apathy like the plague. You will see that apathetic person all over the campus, and he's never done one damn thing for civilization.

"You know, in football, we do learn some wonderful things, and one of them is this. When you get knocked down, which is plenty often, you get right up in a hurry, just as quickly as you can. Then do you know what you do? You probably need more strength. You know where you get it? You get it in a huddle. You get it by going back and getting a new play and running that play together. 'Together' is the thing that gives you the build-up to get ready to go again. And in your lifetime, how well you can work with people will depend on how quickly you get back to them and get together.

"In football, you learn there's nothing that comes easy that's worth a dime. As a matter of fact, I never saw a football player make a tackle with a smile on his face. Never!

"Today, we have a problem with communism. Right now, the communist expects one thing, and you should know this. He expects to conquer the world. And they're tough people. They're just as tough as they can be, and yet we've got to live lives that are better than theirs. The thing they want worst of all right now is what we know so well: computers. Oh, they would love to have our computers, but we can't let them have them. And we're going to have to work probably through another generation to get this settled, if it ever will be. But that's a job that will be in your future.

"And I have no idea, but you may have the attitude and the capacity and the ability to go on from here and help to make this a greater, greater world. And God speed, in the meantime, to all of you!"

When Coach Hayes finished his talk, I was ready to follow him anywhere. Even though I played only one year of freshman football in high school, I wanted to join his team in the worst way ... *I could volunteer to carry the water just to be around the man*, I thought.

I had never had that kind of feeling before, being drawn by the alpha male, the big dog, the great leader, a messianic figure who could produce almost blind loyalty. I thought his team would probably follow him to the edge of the cliff and maybe even into the abyss.

At the breakout sessions during the conference, we had small groups that went through various drills, role-playing, and exercises that were meant to draw out our leadership skills. I received some crazy affirmations in these small group settings, with some of the guys telling me I was going to be President of the United States some day. It was heady stuff to be telling a 21-year-old who had been studying JFK's life and speeches and had suddenly been bitten by the political bug. In the flush of that moment, it seemed like anything and everything was possible.

* * * * * * *

CHAPTER THIRTY-FOUR

AWKWARD ENDINGS, NEW BEGINNINGS

I was surprised to get a call from Laura inviting me to a semi-formal dinner dance organized by her residence hall, where she had become an advisor. I had to carefully guard my feelings. There is something about a first love that is deeply rooted, but with the passage of time I was mostly healed inside. Still, I didn't want to reawaken feelings that could never be returned.

She wore a long satin dress with a plunging neckline, reminding me of Lauren Bacall. We had a good time together, but she felt distant, probably for self-protection. After a few drinks my desire for her began to reawaken. I drove her back to her place, and we went inside. She wore a long coat that covered her beautiful dress.

We sat down on the coach, and I said, "Take off your coat."

"No," she replied firmly.

I reached forward with one hand, but she pushed me away and grabbed the top of her coat with both hands, pulling it tightly around her chest.

It's probably her Christianity that's causing her to act like a prude, I thought to myself. But what could I expect after such a long absence from each other? I was undoubtedly caught up in a foolish fantasy, revealing once more that my carnality was overriding good sense.

Feeling awkward and somewhat pained, I said goodbye and slunk away into the lonely night.

College graduation was fast approaching, and for whatever reason, I could not seem to conjure up any excitement about the occasion. Don Decker came to me and said his family was coming up from southern California to attend the ceremony.

"Is your family coming?" he asked.

"I'm not sure. I've got to check with them. They might be busy ..." my voice trailed off. Sure enough, I called home, and I could tell Mom had no enthusiasm about traveling to Berkeley.

"I'll check with your father, but that's a busy time for us," she said. A couple days later it was official. No one from my family would attend the graduation. So I decided to skip it myself.

After finals, I packed all my clothes and other belongings into a Samsonite suitcase and a few extra boxes. I also took an ancient paddle I dug out of the Fiji garage when we first reclaimed the house and a life preserver one of the boys stole from a restaurant on the waterfront. I loaded everything into my VW Squareback and headed south on Highway 5.

It was the end of one season and the beginning of life in the real world. Despite my faults, failings, ethical and moral compromises, my swelling pride and healthy ego over swayed any negative considerations about my life. On that long, straight drive down the spine of the Golden State, I was remarkably confident, full of boundless enthusiasm for what was within my grasp.

After all, I was living within the sweet spot of America, having grown up in one of its wealthiest zip codes, graduated from one of its most prestigious universities, and led one of the best fraternities on the campus. It's vaunted leadership academy put the icing on my frosty cake of self-congratulation.

My triumph in business, politics, or whatever I put my mind to seemed assured. I would chase success, and become the highest and best version of my own loving self.

* * * * * * *

PART TWO
THE HOUSE ON MOONSAIL

CHAPTER THIRTY-FIVE

FINDING A PATH

My graduation from Berkeley was an emotional let down, partly because nobody in my family was interested enough to make the drive, so I didn't attend the ceremony. Mom and Dad were busy people, with active social lives, and it was a long way from Rolling Hills, California, to Berkeley.

When I got home from college I got the shock of my life. My parents announced they were moving to Orange County, the land of John Wayne, rock-ribbed Republicans, and ticky-tacky suburban sprawl, where developers were paving over every last orange grove, building shopping centers on every corner.

How could Mom and Dad leave their deeply entrenched social world? I discovered Mom was heavily grieving the loss of her tennis coach, Al Fierman, who had died suddenly from a heart attack.

The fact that they were close friends was indisputable, with him giving her a lesson several days a week on the court in our backyard. I wondered if it was more than a friendship, but it seemed impossible that she could be romantically entangled with the much older Jewish man who looked a bit like the woodcarver, Gepetto. He also had a warm, avuncular, lighthearted side that sparked their attachment and emotional connection on and off the court.

At the same time, Dad's business partner, Dick Lane, wanted to relocate from the San Fernando Valley to Rancho Santa Fe in northern San Diego county, an area of sprawling equestrian ranchos for the very wealthy. To accommodate Dick's interests, they settled on a compromise location for a new office, relocating from Westwood village, near UCLA, to San Clemente, the former home of Nixon's Western White House.

Mom and Dad bought a home on a golf course in Orange County in a newly created area called Laguna Niguel, originally part of a land grant from Mexican governor Juan Alvarado to Juan Avila. Following the Mexican-American War, Avila managed to hang on to the three-square league property due to the Treaty of Guadalupe Hidalgo, which honored land grants. One of California's sporadic droughts forced him to sell the property to the Forster family, then it passed to the Moultons, until it wound up in the hands of developers.

Feeling suddenly rootless, I decided to follow Mom and Dad and a vast horde escaping Los Angeles in a phenomenon known as "white flight." The planned move to Orange County felt like a betrayal of everything Berkeley represented. Seeking solace in diversion, I went to see *Heaven Can Wait* with Warren Beatty and Julie Christie.

In the eccentric comedy, Beatty plays an L.A. Rams quarterback, Joe Pendleton, on the verge of making his first appearance in the Super Bowl. As Pendleton rode his bicycle through a tunnel in Malibu, a truck enters from the opposite direction and the driver drifts into the shoulder. Pendleton's guardian angel on first assignment mistakenly believes he is about to die and transports him to heaven, before his time.

A heavenly guide named Mr. Jordan recognizes the blunder and sends Pendleton back to earth in a new body, that of a wealthy industrialist about to be killed by his cheating wife, played by Dyan Cannon. Apparently, Beatty wanted Cary Grant to play Mr. Jordan in the worst way, and used Cannon, Grant's ex-wife, to attempt to lure him out of retirement for the part, but the gambit failed.

CHAPTER THIRTY-FIVE　　　　　　　　　　　FINDING A PATH

Strangely, I fastened on to the peculiarities of Beatty and his film character as role models. I suddenly became obsessed with health food, fitness, collecting zany costumes and his quirky romanticism. I even took a photo of Beatty to my haircutter and asked her to copy the look. Admittedly, Beatty was a long way from the heroes of my dad's generation, mostly laconic World War II vets that displayed sacrificial love in action, refused to speak about their heroism, usually displayed little emotion, and were never braggadocios.

But Beatty became the person I wanted to be and the type of charismatic personality I wanted to project, particularly to women. Dad held the honor of being my first male influencer, then came my first college roommate, Jack, then JFK, and now Beatty. I had to admit it was an odd pantheon of heroes.

Even though Mom and Dad dropped the ball on attending my graduation, they offered a nice consolation gift: a tennis-themed trip to Europe with them. The tour was arranged by a couple of tennis pros in Huntington Beach who set up playing opportunities at private tennis clubs in various European cities, along with tickets to Wimbledon.

Before the trip, however, I went to Brooks Brothers, bought several conservative-looking suits and began interviewing for a real estate job in Newport Beach, ferrying back and forth from Rolling Hills in my parents' Honda Accord. To further complete the fatherly emulation, I purchased two pairs of Wingtip shoes – one black and one brown, full-Brogue Oxford dress shoes with decorative perforations.

Before I started the interviews, dad suggested I get together with several of his contacts in real estate to gather information. I met Burl Warner for lunch, someone dad referred to as "Crazy Burl" because his brilliant business mind, fast-moving tongue, and slashing wit sometimes veered into unexpected terrain.

As we sat across from each other, he started by telling me, "Doing business with your father is like doing business with one of Christ's disciples. If he tells you he's going to do something by a certain date, you can count on it."

Mom had said to me many times, "People trust your father. That's the key to his success." Now Burl was confirming it, and it felt good to know he was held in such high regard, even if this character trait seemed nontransferable, but at least it got me a foot inside the door.

My first real interview was with the manager of Coldwell Banker at a spacious office overlooking the Irvine Industrial Complex. Even though I was dressed conservatively, I still had my longish, curly hair (somewhere between Beatty and Berkeley) and wasn't sure I fit their buttoned-down image, carefully crafted in the vein of IBM salesmen.

"I don't have the resources to train you right now," the manager informed me, which could have been an excuse, or he may not have had a salesman that needed an assistant, sometimes referred to as a runner or gopher. "But with your confidence, you should go a long way."

Later, I ruminated on his comment. Why was I so confident? I harbored the notion that my success was pre-ordained after graduating from Berkeley, leading my college fraternity, and coming from a wealthy, well-connected family. Dad was a big success in real estate; I will be an even bigger success, or so I thought.

Next, I went to Grubb and Ellis, located in a low-rise office building near John Wayne Airport. "You're the son of Don Ellis?" the manager queried.

"Yes, that's my dad," I replied. The manager nodded respectfully. In the last few years, people had confused my dad's real estate company for the better-known firm, led by Harold Ellis, a suave San Francisco real estate leader who loosely resembled the actor Robert Wagner. But this manager seemed to know something about Dad, the "other" Ellis in real estate.

We talked about my motivation for getting into real estate, and he asked how much I wanted to make. "One hundred thousand a year," was my standard reply. It seemed eminently doable, considering Dad had been hitting such numbers since I was in junior high. As I left the interview, the manager said he would get back to me, but a week went by with no phone call.

CHAPTER THIRTY-FIVE — FINDING A PATH

For my next interview, I talked to a lesser-known firm, Ashwill-Burke, started by a couple of go-getting, self-made men. Their office was in a much-less impressive one-story building north of the airport. On the glass entry-door, was a cheap, stick-on sign that read: No Peddlers.

I hit it off immediately with their manager, Dick Petersen, a voluble, barrel-chested, big-grinning man of Swedish extraction, with blonde hair and a ruddy complexion. He let me know they would be moving soon to a new building in a fantastic location with San Diego freeway frontage, next to the MacArthur off-ramp.

He called me a couple days later and said everything looked promising from his end, but he wanted me to come back and meet one of the owners, Gene Ashwill. The next day, I walked into Ashwill's office. The first thing noticeable was a large, prominently displayed photo in vivid color of two pigs kissing. Kansas-bred, he had worked his way through Long Beach State and jumped into real estate with his older brother, Bruce.

It soon became apparent that he was unflinchingly direct, if not a bit coarse. The conversation turned to my father's success, and then he made an unexpected shot across the bow. "I have to tell you," he said, "the sons of successful men usually don't work out."

Since I had a nearly delusional level of self-confidence, I brushed off the comment with an attempt at humor. But after I left his office, the comment festered for a while. Petersen apparently overcame Ashwill's reservations and called the next day to offer me the job. We agreed to a start date of September 1st, which allowed me to have a last summer fling before workaday reality set in.

****

CHAPTER THIRTY-SIX

EUROPEAN TENNIS HOLIDAY, 1978

M om and Dad had taken us to Spain following my graduation from high school, but I had not seen any other parts of Europe, so I looked forward to the trip, even if I would be the only young person traveling with a group of 32 adults mostly over 45-years-old, which seemed ancient to me.

In late June, we boarded a KLM 747 and flew from LAX to Amsterdam, then connected to Gatwick Airport and found our way to the Hogarth Hotel in the Kensington section of London. The next morning our tour guides distributed Wimbledon tickets, along with passes to a private club nearby with grass courts where we could hit balls.

I played on grass for the first time before lunch, which is a completely different experience than concrete. Then I walked into the hallowed grounds of Wimbledon, the venerable home of the All England Lawn Tennis Championships since 1877, the most celebrated tennis tournament in the world. Greeting me were young freckled English girls with beaming moon-faces carrying silver platters piled high with strawberries. It seems the tradition of pairing strawberries and cream dates back to Henry VIII's court. Five hundred years later, the tradition continued in a different court setting, but still bearing the trappings of royalty.

Wimbledon is a curious vestige of British etiquette and propriety, where players are expected to dress modestly in all-whites and bow before the royal box on Centre Court. I left one world in Rolling Hills, California, insulated from the rising tide of L.A.'s multiculturalism, and entered another bubble, also shielded from London's changing face as a vast stream of immigrants from their former colonies began to stream into the city.

When I walked in, I was still wearing my warm-up suit and carrying a racquet and was quickly mobbed by autograph seekers, mistakenly believing I was one of the players. Not wishing to disappoint, I made some illegible chicken scratches on the programs thrust into my face and moved on, chuckling inwardly at the brief moment of mistaken identity.

For someone that had grown up in a tennis household, this was the Mt. Olympus of the genteel sport, where the gods and goddesses of tennis history seemed to hover above the shrine erected to house their memory, with sovereigns spectating from their royal box, surveying the splendor from their dark green Lloyd Loom wicker chairs.

Jimmy Connors beat Vitas Geulaitis to get into the final with Bjorn Borg, the blonde Swedish sensation that made girls swoon. Borg easily won in straight sets for his third Wimbledon title, but before the final, we had already flown off to Amsterdam, where we picked up a rental car and drove to Velp, Holland.

Riding along in our rental car was Mike Franks, Dad's stockbroker, a former child tennis prodigy who played at Beverly Hills High School and later became number one on UCLA's team. Franks talked about his wife Gloria who had not come on the trip but dominated his thoughts from afar. He married the former Goldwyn girl in 1965 after she divorced the songwriter, Sammy Cahn, best known for writing "Three Coins in the Fountain", "High Hopes," and "Call Me Irresponsible" among a number of other hits.

For the last couple of years, Franks organized and ran the Carl Reiner Celebrity Tennis Tournament in La Costa, California. He was somewhat

CHAPTER THIRTY-SIX   EUROPEAN TENNIS HOLIDAY, 1978

intense and insisted on silence in the car when he periodically meditated, instantly entering another dimension as our car sped through the low-level, marshy terrain in Holland.

In Velp, we had matches set for us at the Beekhuizen Club. Velp was very close to Arnhem, the site of a WWII battle dramatized in the film *A Bridge Too Far*, which we had seen recently. Dad was too young for that war, but revered anyone or anything connected to it, so he got very excited by the prospect that we were swinging racquets in the vicinity.

Watching Franks hit balls, I instantly understood why he was a child tennis prodigy. His strokes were the most poetic and fluid of any player I had ever seen. His steely proficiency of shot placement easily bested his opponents, especially in the club matches we had pre-arranged.

From Holland, we drove to Copenhagen, where we had matches arranged at the Kjobenhavns Boldklub, then on to Lyckorna, Sweden, a small hamlet along the coast where we stayed with a doctor and his family in a house once owned by Victor Hasselblad, the camera maker.

The idyllic setting of the Swedish twist on a Victorian house, situated on a promontory overlooking the rocky coast, with a dirt path winding down to the shore instantly became my conception of heaven. There were even wild strawberries one could pluck as they walked along the trail toward the shore.

"I swim in the ocean every day," the good doctor informed us, insisting it was the key to his seemingly robust health.

I left the group in Kristians and departing by ferry to Gothenberg to stay with my college frat brother, Leo Stahlberg. Although he grew up in Finland, his family had relocated to Sweden, which seemed to fit him because he bore a slight resemblance to Bjorn Borg with his long blonde hair and square jaw. I liked trailing along with Leo because he was a chick magnet.

He took me for a run through the woods near his house, but there was no visible trail in sight. I tried to keep up with him as he moved through the rough terrain with the ease of a pentathalete. We were jumping across small streams, leaping and clambering over boulders, racing through thickets with dense growth, swatting branches away from our faces.

Leo came up with the idea of the two of us doing an over-nighter in Denmark, so we took a ferry across the North Sea to Frederikshavn on the Jutland Peninsula. He knew about a place along the coast where there were abandoned German bunkers from World War II, with their cannons still in place. It was a spectacular setting that excited the imagination as we blew past the signs that said, "Closed to the public," and climbed into the massive concrete structures. It was a bit eerie to see the big guns designed by the House of Krupp and consider what it would be like to be stationed there during the war. Ghosts from the past seemed to be floating around us, which made me uneasy.

In a throwback to our college days, we proceeded to get sloshed at one of the local establishments, drinking too many Danish and Belgian beers. It's been said that wine is a mocker and beer is a brawler, and the stroppy side of Leo, which hearkened back to our frat days, began to emerge after six or seven beers. He got very boisterous and knocked over a sign on the way back to our cheap hotel. I didn't like the prospect of getting arrested in a foreign country, and was relieved when we both passed out in our room.

* * * * * * *

CHAPTER THIRTY-SEVEN
RELOCATION

I moved into one of the spare bedrooms at Mom and Dad's house they purchased on the 18th fairway at El Niguel Country Club. They joined the golf club and the tennis club nearby, the latter owned by Peter Paxton, one of the tennis players on the Europe trip.

Paxton, always tan and fit, had just sold the Carmel Valley Racquet Club, which he founded a decade earlier. It attracted celebrities like Dinah Shore and Merv Griffin, along with Stan Smith, the Grand Slam singles champion from Pasadena who also became known for his line of Adidas shoes.

It was a five-minute walk to the tennis club and it quickly became my hangout on the weekends and in off hours. After hitting balls with Mom one afternoon, an older woman at the club offered to buy me a beer. I immediately sensed this attractive wife of a local real estate magnate had a thing about younger guys. Even though she was beautiful, I had no thought of getting involved with a woman 10 or more years older.

When I started work with Ashwill-Burke, I wasn't sure about what I would be doing. They put six or eight of the new recruits through a two-day training program. Two days? It seemed woefully inadequate to me.

I soon learned I would be hitting the streets, cold calling, trying to establish myself in an assigned geographical area. Even though the sign on the front door said "No Peddlers," I realized that all my compatriots were glorified peddlers of commercial real estate.

Each of the agents had a cubicle slightly larger than a five-foot desk, a four-foot-high, square, walled enclosure. In the cubicle adjacent to me was Uri Gantz, who arrived a few months before the current manager took over. Uri did not fit the mold of Orange County a bit. He had hair to his shoulders and dressed like he still had one foot in the hippie movement, rejecting the buttoned-down, conservative look of most of the guys.

It was rumored that before the previous manager left the company with a few of the top salespeople, he made a few unconventional hires to sandbag the owners of the company.

Uri grew up in a Jewish family in Brentwood, a tiny suburb in West L.A., with a Jewish father successful in real estate. He graduated from Berkeley in 1968, exactly a decade before me. Uri was part of the protest movement and imbibed deeply of the drug culture at Berkeley. To avoid Vietnam, he continued his studies at Columbia in New York, where he became attracted to Eastern religion.

After he dropped out of Columbia, he lived on the streets briefly and then went to stay in an ashram, where he met his current wife. Our lives paralleled in a few ways, with the Berkeley connection, fathers in real estate, and an affinity for Eastern mysticism. I accepted an invitation to his apartment for dinner. He had sawn the legs off their dining room table, so we could sit around the table on pillows strewn on the floor.

They had a toddler in the house and made their own vegetarian baby food in the blender from what we were having for dinner, sort of a mock beef stew with lots of tofu, carrots, and potatoes.

Uri and I hit it off, and I loved him, partly because he was such a misfit with the culture of Orange County and the company where we worked, in addition to having a wry manner that mimicked George Carlin. Sadly, he did not last very long, and I soon had a seasoned salesman sitting next to me named Nick. Nick was a smoothie, dressed impeccably

CHAPTER THIRTY-SEVEN — RELOCATION

in finely tailored expensive suits, and drove a Mercedes convertible.

He arranged a tennis match with me, his wife, and stepdaughter at the Newport Beach Tennis Club. Nick's second wife, Mandy, was beautiful and quite a few years younger. Nick got mad at me at one point in the match when his daughter and I were receiving serves from Nick's wife, Mandy. I called one of her first serves "wide," which he took exception to, and lambasted me in a scowling, derisive tone.

"Don't stand on the service line and call my shots wide!" he barked. I took his point that from my vantage point, I could more easily judge if his serves were long, rather than wide, but his flash of anger about the issue seemed extreme.

Later, I was at a friend's house for dinner, and when I brought up Nick's name, they reacted negatively. It seems he had "stolen" their unsuspecting friend's wife at the same club where we played. He told me that Nick had been spending a lot of time at the club and began to make moves on their friend while her husband was working. Tennis was a "love" game in more than its scoring methodology.

I soon learned the racquet club near our new house was developing a reputation for having a number of couples with very fluid marriages. There was wife swapping and marriages breaking apart right and left, along with hot tub parties in private homes that were "clothing optional" affairs.

A few days later, Nick startled me with his directness when I first arrived at the office. "What happened to you last night? Did you get beat up?"

"Oh, I don't know. I probably didn't have a good night's sleep," I said sheepishly. It was the first indication that my boyish good looks were fading fast, and excesses of food, alcohol, and lack of sleep were taking their toll.

I hit it off with the receptionist at Ashwill-Burke, an attractive and voluptuous brunette named Ricki with a 1000-watt smile, even if that wattage didn't extend to the upper cortical regions. She was married to a hypnotist, which caused my devilish imagination to run wild because her "wakeful state" seemed pretty loose and uninhibited.

When I arrived in the office on a typical Monday, after a weekend of surfing, tennis, and lying on the beach, she would start cooing about my deep tan. "How do you get a tan like that?" she wanted to know. "It's so even."

In truth, I hardly ever used sunscreen. Only when snow skiing in the mountains would I put a little Sea and Ski on my nose. The whole idea was to bake as dark as possible, sometimes using coconut oil to magnify the sun's burning rays. Occasionally, I would use another Coppertone product called "Shade," which had a sun-protection factor of six.

When calls came into the Ashwill-Burke office, Ricki was supposed to route them to the agent who held the listing connected with the sign on the property. Due to our budding friendship, and the fact that I was one of the few salespeople in the office at the time, she *mistakenly* put a call through to me from another agent's listing in North Orange County, miles away from my assigned area in South County.

"This is Howard Williams with Pattiport Industries," the man began, with a strong Texas twang. "I'm looking for a building in Anaheim of about 50,000 square feet. I saw the sign and wondered if you could help me out?"

"Yes, absolutely," I bluffed. I had never even been inside a 50,000 square foot industrial building. Just getting my start, I was attempting to find tenants that would lease buildings in the 1,500 to 3,000 square foot range.

A few days later, Howard arrived at our new office fronting on the San Diego Freeway. The minute he saw me his countenance dropped; I could see visible disappointment register on his face. He immediately sized me up as a long-haired "kid" with little experience, which was true.

He was relieved when he found out my manager, Dick, would be accompanying us on our building tour in Anaheim.

When we first walked into a 50,000 square foot building, larger than a football field, I was in awe. With Dick's steady guidance, Howard felt confident to make an offer on one of the buildings we toured, to my delight.

CHAPTER THIRTY-SEVEN — RELOCATION

In the midst of the negotiations, Mom and Dad invited me to spend a weekend with them at a condo they had just purchased in Palm Springs, within walking distance of The Tennis Club, the former haunt of Hollywood legends that by the late 70s was fading a bit.

They invited another couple and their daughter, and I quickly recognized this to be a set-up. Dr. Gary, an anesthesiologist, and his wife, Dorothy, were tennis friends of my parents through the Jack Kramer Club in Rolling Hills Estates. They had a very bright and attractive blonde daughter who was a senior at Stanford. I took her out once when I was home from Berkeley during the summer, but I never followed-up because we were in different orbits. But I was definitely interested now.

* * * * * * *

CHAPTER THIRTY-EIGHT

IN THE HUNT

I drove out to Palm Springs directly from work on a Friday, fighting the traffic on the 91 freeway in my Honda Accord, and arrived at the condo near Patencio and Baristo. When I walked in, I had on dark brown dress pants, a powder blue cotton oxford buttoned-down shirt, and a brown tie. The doctor and his wife arrived shortly after that, and Jamie and I seemed to hit it off right away.

The next day, we played tennis together and went swimming. I got a call from Howard Williams with Pattiport. We discussed elements of the deal and where the negotiations should go. Jamie overheard the conversation, which inflated my ego a bit. *I must be important since I'm involved in big deals*, I thought.

Later in the afternoon, we were lounging on the couch in the living room. She had her shoes off and was wearing short white tennis socks. For some strange reason, short white socks on women were a turn-on to me. Her shapely legs were folded up on the couch, with her feet a few inches away.

"Do you like foot rubs?" I asked, moving my hand over to the sole of her foot and beginning to rub the soft cotton.

"Oh, yes. Everybody likes foot rubs," she replied, to my delight. We had not had any physical contact up to this point, but the foot rub broke the ice.

That evening, Jamie and I had dinner with the parents and then went to see *Superman*, which turned out to be a surprisingly romantic movie.

I had grown up with the old TV series, *The Adventures of Superman*, filmed from 1952 to 1958, with Superman played by George Reeves. After being weaned off the *Mickey Mouse Club*, Superman was my first TV hero, and I got wrapped up in his quest for truth, justice, and the American way. It inculcated the strong view that good must always triumph over criminality and evil, and a magical, superhuman solution to malfeasance would always present itself in the 11th hour, the last five to ten minutes of the program.

Reeves died in 1959 at only 45 years old, from a single gunshot wound to the head, with the death labeled a suicide. It was said that he was depressed about being typecast as Superman in the public eye, which made it difficult for him to find serious roles.

There were a few strange twists to his death, however, which caused some to say his death was not a suicide. He was found in the upstairs bedroom of his home in Benedict Canyon by partygoers downstairs, which included his newly minted fiancée and three others. They said they only heard one shot fired, but three bullets were discharged from the .30 caliber Lugar found at his feet. Authorities could find no fingerprints on the gun and there was no gunpowder residue on his hands.

Reeves had a long-time affair with Toni Mannix, the wife of MGM's general manager and "fixer," Eddie Mannix. Apparently, Eddie did not care so much about the affair, which was an open secret, because he was involved in an affair himself with a Japanese woman. But Reeves had dumped Toni for another woman, and Toni became the woman scorned, distraught, and enraged, which upset the equilibrium of the Mannix house, especially after Reeves and his new flame announced they would marry.

Reeves' mother didn't buy the suicide conclusion, and a second autopsy was ordered, which found bruises on his head and body of unknown origin. Because of Eddie's rumored ties to the mob, it was thought he (or his wife) might have ordered the hit. An L.A. publicist claimed that Toni erected a shrine to Reeves in her home and regularly asked God and Reeves for forgiveness during prayer sessions he witnessed and that she even confessed to her involvement in his death with a Catholic priest.

The new Superman featured Christopher Reeve in the lead role. The similarity in the names immediately struck me, but Reeve turned out to be even more winsome than Reeves, with a face as "strong and sharp as an axe blade," according to *Newsweek*. A remarkable list of A-list actors turned down the part, including Robert Redford, Paul Newman, and Burt Reynolds. Olympic champion Bruce Jenner and weight lifting phenomenon Arnold Schwarzenegger tried out for the part but were rejected. Two hundred unknowns were auditioned, including producer Ilya Salkind's wife's dentist.

Initially, they thought Reeve was too thin for the role, but he went on a crash weight lifting and high-protein diet and gained 25 pounds of upper body strength. The surprising part of the film turned out to be the romance between Lois Lane, played by Margot Kidder, and Superman. Their tête-à-tête on the balcony of her penthouse apartment overlooking Metropolis, aka New York City, at night, followed by him taking her into his arms for a dream-like flight over the city lights, set the perfect tone for the remainder of the evening.

We drove from the old theater on Palm Canyon back to the condo and discovered our parents had already retired for the evening. They left on some soft lighting in the living room. We stood next to the couch. I grabbed her hand, then sat down and pulled her onto my lap, facing away from me. I started to kiss her on the back of the neck, then slung her around to face me.

"I thought that was going to be interesting," she said coyly. We stretched ourselves out on the soft white denim couch, kept our clothes on, considering our parents were in the next room, and had a very intense make out session, buoyed by a tide of romantic feeling sparked by Lois and Clark.

When I returned to the office on Monday, the gigantic lease deal came together quickly. I learned there is a certain momentum to a real estate transaction, and if I happened to be in the middle of it, even though I had little experience or knowledge, it would happen. With a major assist from my office manager, I walked away with a commission check for $15,000. Everyone in the office celebrated, except for the sales team who should have received the lead when the phone call first came into the office. They were not happy and complained to my manager, but I was oblivious, basking in my first success.

A few weeks later we had our annual Christmas dinner, and I received an award as "Rookie of the Year."

* * * * * * *

CHAPTER THIRTY-NINE

SURFING AT SALT CREEK

To celebrate my deal, I bought a white Audi 5000 and a new surfboard from Hobie Sports in Dana Point. The seven-foot, nine-inch board had fairly thick rails and was shaped by Terry Martin, a legendary shaper in the area.

Martin shaped his first 10-foot board when he was only 14, using some balsa wood he found in a scrap pile. His first board was lighter, sleeker, faster, and more maneuverable than the typical "logs" out there, and there was instant demand. He could shape wood or foam the way Michelangelo worked with marble, and he went on to shape some 80,000 boards.

On my first trip to Salt Creek in September 1978, there was a mild Santa Ana wind condition, with warm air blowing from the desert toward the coast, so the water was glassy, with about three or four-foot waves generated from the south wrapping around a rocky point.

The sand was billowy white, the water clear and clean. There were not many people on the beach or in the water. When I paddled out at the point, I could look down and see the water was teeming with fish. It was like Hawaii! I couldn't believe I would be living in such a place.

After only a week of using the new board, the leash that connected the board to my ankle snapped on a large wave, sending the board crashing over the rocks at the point. I swam in to retrieve the board and discovered Terry Martin's beautiful glass job was now punctured by at least 20 or 30 jagged holes. It was sad because I knew that even if I repaired the dings, the board would never be the same.

When the weather turned cold, my thoughts turned to skiing, and I concocted a plan for a ski weekend at Lake Tahoe with Jamie. I knew my parents' friends, Dick and Barbie Racich, had a beautiful cabin at Tahoe City with a commanding view of the lake. Audaciously, I called them and essentially invited Jamie and me to stay with them.

Jamie was a senior at Stanford at the time, so I flew into San Jose airport, rented a car, picked her up at school, and then we wound our way out Highway 80 to the Racich cabin.

Dick and Barbie met in Boulder as students at the University of Colorado, where Dick played football and majored in physics. He taught physics for a while and then jumped into real estate, where he had done well. The best thing he ever did was marry Barbie, a tall, slender blonde with a love of adventure that almost matched his. They enjoyed all ocean, lake, and mountain sports and traveled the world together, seeking new adventures. If I could pick an alternative set of parents, they would be high on the list.

They kept their house at a crisp 55 degrees, which seemed relatively comfortable in the winter. Barbie gave us a tour of the house, which included a loom where she wove large, 60s-style wall hangings. Dick had his office at the top of the house with a jaw-dropping view of the lake from his desk. Barbie showed Jamie and me to a downstairs bonus room, pulled me aside, and asked,

"Is it okay with your mother if you two sleep in the same room?"

"Oh, yeah. It's no problem," I assured her, not completely sure if Mom would approve, but we were in sleeping bags, which seemed innocent.

Jamie and I got along well that weekend, skiing at Squaw Valley and Alpine Meadows, but it seemed like a brother and sister relationship because our families had known each other so long. While I was enthusiastic, a spark seemed to be lacking on her side.

On Sunday, we drove back to Stanford, and I spent the night in her dorm room. There was light romance, but as I flew home, I wasn't very confident the relationship would go anywhere.

* * * * * * *

CHAPTER FORTY

A TOWNHOUSE BY THE BEACH

After my first year post-college living with my parents, Dad came to me and delivered a harsh dose of reality. It was time to move out on my own. They knew I had some money in my pocket from my first big real estate deal, so the time seemed propitious to make a move.

I met a young real estate agent named Shepard "Shep" Daniels as he walked through our neighborhood passing our flyers. We immediately hit it off, so I decided to go out looking for property with him. Shep came from a prominent family in Florida and someone told me he and his sister were chauffeured to school in a limo. I liked his mild, honey-infused southern drawl and his affable, sincere nature. His southern charm might be valuable in negotiating with home sellers, I thought.

We went out driving around and looked at several properties. Almost immediately, I liked a small, 900 square foot townhome he showed me in Niguel Shores, a private, gated community that straddled Pacific Coast Highway near Salt Creek, my favorite surfing spot.

The property was about a 10-minute walk to the beach and had a tiny ocean view if some oleander bushes were trimmed properly. It had white shag carpet throughout, woodsy-looking paneling in the living room, along with a pot-belly stove fireplace. The master bedroom had cheap, walnut paneling and deep red velvet drapes that gave it a bordello feel.

The homeowner was asking $125,000 for the place, and we offered $110,000. I had $15,000 saved for the down payment, and Mom and Dad loaned me an additional $10,000.

After we struck a deal at $112,000, Shep and I went back for a more thorough property inspection. I met the owner, Jim, a 40-ish high school teacher whose passion was volleyball. He played at the beach frequently and had a handsome, rugged, weathered look to him. I was surprised when he told me his girlfriend was 19 and his former student.

"It's kind of a drag because we can't really go out in public," he confided. "We didn't start the relationship until after she graduated and turned 18, but still, it's touchy, and I could get in trouble."

I applied for a loan but had concerns about qualifying, since my job was based on commissions only, an irregular source of income. A loan officer at Security Pacific Bank breezily told me to make up a number, extrapolating an annual income from my recent deal.

It was a hot real estate market in Southern California. Because of rampant inflation, partly caused by government spending, everything was going up. It confirmed my Berkeley econ prof's definition of inflation: *too many dollars chasing too few goods*. Making money in California housing seemed like a no-brainer, so the banks were lending freely.

As Shep and I drove together on Crown Valley Parkway down a long stretch with giant eucalyptus trees, he surprised me by inviting me to attend a Christian singles group at Mariners Church in Newport Beach.

It was a bright, sunlit day, but when he brought up this Christian group, the interior of his car seemed to get brighter, filling with an other-worldly glow.

"I went to the group before I got married," he told me. "It's a large gathering, and they meet at a food court in Irvine, Plaza de Cafes. I don't go, but I could ask a friend of mine, Barry VanFleet, to go with you and introduce you to people."

Barry VanFleet!!?? I exclaimed inwardly. He was the son of a promi-

CHAPTER FORTY

nent real estate developer in Orange County and had recently made a presentation at my company about a massive retail center they were building in Laguna Niguel, patterned after a highly successful retail center they built in L.A.

I had no interest in God, but forging any kind of connection with Barry could only benefit my real estate career. And maybe I would meet some single women a few notches higher in quality than the ones I met in bars.

"Yes, I'd like to go," I told Shep.

"Good. I'll have Barry give you a call."

As Shep and I parted, I suddenly realized my carefree lifestyle would soon have a mortgage payment attached to it, property taxes and homeowner's insurance to pay, grass to mow and bushes to trim. Life was getting more serious, but perhaps this singles group would provide the social diversion I needed.

Barry called me a few days later, and we met at a Chevron station on Crown Valley Parkway. Churchill remarked that when he first met FDR, it was like uncorking a bottle of champagne. The same could be said for my first meeting with Barry, easily the most effervescent, warm, authentically impressive 25-year-old I had met in my life.

This guy could be governor some day, or President, I thought. I followed him to the singles group in my Audi 5000. He was driving a Lincoln Town Car of some sort of special early numbered vintage from the assembly line, made for his father or uncle.

We hit it off right away, and he began introducing me around the group, about 300 singles, with many beautiful women from affluent families in Orange County. Many of the guys were bookish, pale, engineering types with snail-darter personalities. I couldn't believe my good fortune.

The leader of the group, Mike Riegle, led an informal church service, preaching a message that went in one ear and out the other. I couldn't really focus on it. I was too mesmerized and bedazzled by my bright prospects in this new social world. God was not on my radar, but scores of attractive blondes and brunettes had my sudden attention.

In the fall, they held a talent show at a school auditorium in Corona Del Mar. For a group of Christians, they seemed to know how to have fun, with many skits inspired by *Saturday Night Live*, like the "Wide Bottoms," with Barry and friends performing a very believable rendition of the big booty pranksters. There were gross moments, like the spoof about hawking a blender on late-night TV, Bass-O-Matic, demonstrating the product by throwing a dead fish inside as the motor whirred and the squishy entrails swooshed around the inside of the glass container.

Dixie Spratt, a vivacious sorority girl that graduated from USC, did an incredible portrayal of Lily Tomlin from Rowan and Martin's *Laugh-In* playing a phone operator in the sketch: "One Ringy Dingy."

I got up to do my impression of Jimmy Stewart reading the Robert Frost poem, "Stopping by Woods on a Snowy Evening." Since I was about 17, I discovered an ability to do impressions of people, and Jimmy Stewart was my first to gain notice and approval. After a fashion, I could credibly do Cary Grant, Clark Gable, JFK jawing with his brother Teddy, FDR, Jimmy Carter, and others.

Where this gift came from is a complete mystery to me, but it just seemed to show up one day, a strange facility seemingly plucked from some higher intelligence in the cosmos, perhaps.

When the talent show ended, I worked my way through the crowd of people to meet Dixie Spratt and gushed over her performance. I got her phone number and soon had my first date from the Christian singles group.

* * * * * * *

In November, Americans were shocked when Iranian students had the temerity to take over the American embassy in Tehran and hold 50 American diplomats hostage. It was a poke in the eye of President Jimmy Carter and the rest of the country and made him appear feckless when he couldn't resolve the situation quickly.

After I got through the holidays, I held the first party at my new digs,

CHAPTER FORTY — A TOWNHOUSE BY THE BEACH

sending out a hand-drawn invitation for an "American Hostage Costume Party," reflecting my perverse humor. The instructions said to wear the native dress of the foreign country of your choice. The slogan for the gathering was "Remember The Hostages." At the top of the invite, I drew a turtle with four small elephants on its back upholding the top half of the globe and two American flags hanging limply to either side.

On the sides of the inside page of the invitation, I drew the faces of the Ayatollah Khomeini, an Egyptian pharaoh, Napoleon, Queen Elizabeth, and other foreign dignitaries, suggesting people might wear "kimonos, fezes, turbans, or tunics, loincloths, ruffles, bustles, and hoops, boleros, breeches, serapes and kilts, togas, MuuMuus, or birthday suits."

There was a great turnout for the party; Barry VanFleet showed up with a friend from his Coast Guard days in his dress uniform, sporting a phenomenal beard, meticulously trimmed in Edwardian fashion. There was a group from my UCLA connection because I lived in the Sigma Nu house in Westwood during the summer before my senior year at Cal.

There were a few glitches of my own making, however. I converted the garage to a disco and had painted a huge banner on one wall. Unfortunately, the paint was still wet, so anyone who happened to lean in that direction got paint on their outfit.

I was dateless, and as the night wore on, I started dancing with the wife of an attendee I didn't know well, but they had connections to the UCLA group. As Earth, Wind and Fire's song "Reasons" played, I had a very exuberant dance with this fellow's wife, which provoked a jealous response in him. I should have known better. I was wearing a Spanish bullfighter's outfit with tight-fitting pants and probably came off as a Latin philanderer from his perspective as the two of us sashayed around the floor in a tightly swinging and swaying embrace. Suddenly, he was the bull, his eyes glaring at me, his nostrils snorting, ready to charge. We ended the dance, and I quickly backed away, but the damage was done.

Late in the afternoon a few weeks later, I got some devastating news as I drove north on the San Diego Freeway in Costa Mesa. KABC news reported the body of a man had been recovered who jumped off the Vincent Thomas Bridge in San Pedro. They identified the man as Robert Fawell, 24, my best childhood friend from the fourth grade through my freshman year in high school.

I knew he had been depressed and attempted suicide at least once. The son of a medical doctor and his deeply religious Lutheran wife, "Bobby," as I knew him, was one of the most well-liked and popular kids at our school. After high school, he lost his way and entered a dark night of the soul that never relented. His father made sure he got the best pharmaceuticals, but they slowed him down and dulled his vibrant personality. When I last saw him, he was a shadow of the bright spark I once knew. He complained he didn't like life on the drugs, and he didn't like reality when he was off the drugs.

After Bobby took his life, his mother could not open the pages of her Bible for more than a year.

Occasionally, I read *Good News for Modern Man*, a paraphrase of the Bible in contemporary language given to me by my mother. But mostly, my go-to book for spiritual solace was *Be Here Now*, by Ram Dass, the former Harvard professor and pal of Timothy Leary who had fully embraced Eastern religion. His book had become the third-ranked bestseller after the Bible and Benjamin Spock.

* * * * * *

CHAPTER FORTY-ONE

SALT COMPANY SKI TRIP

I signed up for a ski trip to Mammoth Mountain with the Christian singles group. *What would it be like to spend a weekend with these religious types?* I wondered. I had purchased a new pair of Dynastar Omeglass skis and new boots, so I relished the chance to get back on the slopes following my Aspen sojourn. Dynastar Omeglass were considered hot skis; the company grew out of a merger between Dynamic and Starcraft.

The bus trip up Highway 395 was uneventful. I ended up in a three-bedroom condo near the ski slopes with Dixie Spratt, the Lily Tomlin impressionist, Barry VanFleet, and his new girlfriend he met in the group, Dorie Denton. I shared a room with Bill Carter, the son of one of L.A.'s most powerful and influential businessmen, the founder and CEO of a prominent department store chain.

Before the trip, I had one date with Dixie Spratt, and while it didn't go anywhere, we had a great chemistry from the standpoint of a budding friendship. She was suddenly interested in a tall, handsome guy from Colorado, Dave Brandenberg. He and Dixie became inseparable on the ski trip.

A massive snowstorm descended on the Sierras that weekend. I attempted to go out on Saturday morning, took a couple runs in blizzard conditions, fell, got wet, couldn't see more than a few feet ahead of my skis in the whiteout conditions at the top of the lift, and finally gave up.

That night, before we nodded off to sleep, Bill and I got into a deeper conversation about spiritual matters. He seemed to question whether or not I was really a Christian and began to probe me in earnest.

"Would you say there is one way to God?" he asked.

"I've always believed there are many pathways to God," I replied, based on my limited study of world religions and because of the strong influence of Ram Dass and his book, *Be Here Now*. It seemed logical to me that there was a kernel of truth in all these various systems of belief that led ultimately to the same place.

"But Jesus said, 'I am the way and the truth and life, no one comes to the Father but through me,' " Bill said.

I knew Ram Dass had an explanation for that verse in his book, but I couldn't remember exactly his interpretation. In any event, the exclusivity of Christianity was a stumbling block I couldn't quite get my head around.

We fell asleep without resolving anything, but I had a feeling that Bill harbored suspicions about my underlying beliefs.

After another snow day with little skiing, we packed up for the bus ride home. As we were packing, Bill started singing the Bobby Darin song from the Sixties, "Mack the Knife." I had never heard the song before, but the lyrics were hilarious, to the extent he could recall them.

Oh, the shark, babe,
Has such teeth, dear
And he shows them,
Pearly white.
Just a jackknife
Has old macheath, babe,
And he keeps it, ahh
Out of sight.

CHAPTER FORTY-ONE   SALT COMPANY SKI TRIP

Bill and I sat together on the bus, and we had great fun as he worked at recalling more of the lyrics, and I wrote them down on the back of a party invitation. It was said on the day of Pentecost that all of Jesus' disciples appeared to be drunk, and to the people around us on the bus, we must have appeared to be under the influence of something as we laughed and sang our way down Highway 395, bellowing out the words to this inane song with delight.

We stopped for food in Bishop at Schat's Bakery and Kentucky Fried Chicken. When we resumed the journey, Barry and Dorie, and Dixie and Dave joined our zany songfest, but we began to substitute our own made-up lyrics, trying to outdo each other with our merry madness.

At the end of the trip, I had to revise my impression of Christians. I had thought of them as dour killjoys, narrow, buttoned-up, without much capacity to enjoy life fully. We had such fun that our smaller group within the group began to call ourselves "the skidoos." What surprised me is that I didn't even get stoned or loaded to have a good time, and this trip was one of the best of my life, despite the terrible ski conditions.

****

CHAPTER FORTY-TWO

THE PRESIDENTIAL CAMPAIGN OF 1980

When I graduated from Berkeley, I wasn't sure if I was a Democrat or a Republican. I registered Republican and voted for Ford in 1976, primarily due to my parents' influence. Since then, all my political heroes had become Democrats, such as JFK, FDR, and to a lesser extent, Truman.

Because of my economics courses at Cal, I was a fiscal conservative. But as a result of my biology courses in high school and media influences, I was very pro-abortion, believing excess population to be the greatest threat to the world. Something in the water in Orange County seemed to pull me in a more conservative direction, but I couldn't abide Ronald Reagan, the B-movie actor and former governor, thinking his lack of Washington experience and lightweight image would be a disaster.

Sadly, Jimmy Carter's presidency was becoming the butt of late-night comedians' jokes, and his handling of the hostage crisis in Iran had diminished America's standing in the world. He also got blamed for long gas lines during the energy crisis, which brought back painful memories from 1973.

I first took notice of John Anderson at a Republican candidates' debate in Des Moines, Iowa, that included Reagan, George H.W. Bush, Phil Crane, and Anderson. The silver-haired, articulate congressman from Rockford, Illinois, separated himself from the other Republicans on stage by stating that reducing taxes, increasing defense spending, and balancing the budget would never work.

My econ classes at Berkeley had taught me as much. So when he cast off the Republicans after a strong showing in the primaries and decided to run as an independent, I went to an organizing meeting in Orange County for his campaign.

About a dozen people showed up for the meeting held in the candle-lit living room of a modest home owned by a single woman in Costa Mesa. It soon became apparent as we went around the room that nobody really wanted to run the campaign. Some held positions in Orange County government or affiliations with other parties, so they didn't want to be publicly identified with Anderson's renegade campaign.

At 24, with abundant energy and enthusiasm, wearing a suit, and asking semi-intelligent questions, their eyes fell on me. "Will you do it?" asked Dinah, a government employee.

Without thinking about how I would juggle my full-time job in real estate with running a countywide presidential campaign, I said yes. When everyone filtered out of the house, I found myself alone with the home-owner, who was a lonely woman in her early thirties. Rebuffing her invitation to stay and get acquainted in the warm glow of a dozen candles burning, I beat a hasty retreat, wondering what I had gotten myself into.

I found an old house to rent on North Broadway in Santa Ana, just above the civic center, that became the headquarters of our "National Unity Campaign." Largely composed of Democrats disillusioned with Carter, our leadership team included Ken and Dinah, congenial public servants; a sharp-tongued liberal activist named Arlene; an astute young attorney named Steven; and a young woman I met during the summer I lived in the Sigma Nu house at UCLA, Reese Sandeberg.

It soon became apparent that women would form the backbone of our volunteer force, especially those who did not work or only worked part-

CHAPTER FORTY-TWO   THE PRESIDENTIAL CAMPAIGN OF 1980

time. For the first time in my life, I got involved with two female volunteers at the same time, a completely untenable situation on every level.

Reese had a disarmingly sweet manner that belied a razor-sharp intelligence. After taking the bar exam, she was applying to law schools and would depart for Hastings Law School in the fall of 1980. She had long, straight, blonde hair pulled back into a ponytail and a glorious physique honed by her steady advancement in ballet. She also had a tall, handsome boyfriend from UCLA intent on making the PGA tour. They were supposedly engaged, and she happened to be living in a spare bedroom at his parents' house in a private, gated beach community.

One night, Reese stayed late to help me with a project. All the other volunteers had left, and we found ourselves alone. I turned on some music, and suddenly, we were dancing in the middle of campaign headquarters, surrounded by clunky desks and boxes and papers strewn about. The dancing turned into a long, slow kiss and the start of an affair to remember.

I took her out to my parents' condo in Palm Springs, and we spent a Saturday afternoon hiking in Tahquitz canyon among the pools and waterfalls, plunging into the cool, clear water running down the granitic San Jacinto Mountains, rising steeply above the desert floor, forced upward by the San Andreas fault. Since I was in elementary school, experts had been talking about The Big One hitting somewhere around here because this section of the fault last went off a couple hundred years ago and pressure has been building ever since.

But we were oblivious to any such threats, which Californians learn to live with, as we blithely splashed in the pools and tanned our bodies on rocks warmed by the desert sun.

One weekend, after a campaign event, Reese came to my townhouse in Niguel Shores, and we found ourselves naked on the white shag carpet in my bedroom. Influenced by Bernardo Bertolucci's film, *Last Tango in Paris*, I attempted to recreate the position displayed on posters publicizing the movie, with actor Marlon Brando facing co-star Maria Schneider, sitting on the floor. I was one of many transfixed by Vittorio

Storaro's cinematography, "shot in orangey hues and blond browns inspired by Francis Bacon's paintings, which gave the movie's eroticism an artistic air," according to reviewers.

The color of light in Bacon's paintings reminded Bertolucci of Paris in the winter, when "the lights of the stores are on, and there is a very beautiful contrast between the leaden gray of the wintry sky and the warmth of the show windows ... the light in the paintings was the major source of inspiration for the style we were looking for," Bertolucci told biographer Ciaretta Tonetti.

Behind the beautiful pastiche, however, there was a dark underbelly. Bertolucci sprung a rape scene on 19-year-old Maria Schneider without informing her until the day the scene was shot. She protested mightily when she discovered the deception, throwing things around the set. While the sex was simulated in the scene that famously used butter as an improvised lubricant, Schneider actually felt violated, and her tears were real.

In the film, it doesn't work out so well between Marlon Brando's character and the character played by Schneider. That moment also became the turning point in my relationship with Reese, who began to pull away from the campaign that summer as she prepared to leave for law school.

Meanwhile, I got myself entangled with another female staffer named Linda, a long-legged creature with a beautiful face, who stood about two inches taller than me. We and a couple other volunteers set up a booth at the Orange County fair and handed out campaign literature, bright-red bumper stickers, and buttons. Then we went back to Linda's apartment and found ourselves thrashing around in her bedroom.

After our encounter, she said, "I get so close with you." In my naiveté, I wasn't exactly sure what she meant and didn't want to guess about something I had never actually witnessed.

I soon found myself in some awkward situations, with Reese and Linda showing up at the same campaign activities before Reese left for school. How could I have been so foolish as to put myself in this delicate situation? It made me incredibly nervous to make excuses and bend the

CHAPTER FORTY-TWO — THE PRESIDENTIAL CAMPAIGN OF 1980

Mark Ellis with Presidential Candidate, John Anderson, 1980

truth to avoid one or the other finding out I was cheating. After Reese departed, I breathed a sigh of relief, but learned a valuable lesson about two-timing that I did not want to repeat in the future.

Anderson made a fleeting campaign stop in L.A. to raise money from the Hollywood elite on the West Side, and we trooped up to meet him and have a quick photo taken with the silver-haired gentleman, at this point looking somewhat haggard from the nonstop demands of a presidential campaign. His eyes were vacant as he met our leadership team, and we crowded around him for the photo op. Our two-minute interaction as a group could not have been more unsatisfying, but we probably should not have expected anything more.

As the campaign wore on, our hopes that Anderson would go above his 10 to 15 percent poll numbers were all pinned to our expectation that he would blow away the field when it came time for presidential debates with Reagan and Carter. Our anticipation began to build during the summer of 1980, but something unexpected and unnerving happened closer to home.

* * * * * * *

CHAPTER FORTY-THREE

MURDER BY THE SEA

Living in a gate-guarded community near the beach, crime was about the farthest thing from my mind. I never locked the door to my townhouse, figuring a thief wouldn't really want my old black and white, boxy, Zenith TV or my crummy stereo.

On the Sunday night I returned from Palm Springs with Reese, I got a surprise when I opened the front door of my place and walked in. There, sitting on the coffee table next to the couch was a tall can of Colt 45 beer, completely consumed except for a bit of swill in the bottom of the can.

Who walked into my place while I was in Palm Springs? None of my friends drank Colt 45. It was the stuff of bikers and brawlers, bad-ass dudes with something to prove about their machismo.

Nothing was missing from my house, so I threw the can in the trash and didn't think a whole lot about it. Out of habit more than anything else, I continued to keep my place unlocked.

A couple of weeks later, I woke up to the startling news that a young newlywed couple, Keith and Patti Harrington, had been murdered two streets away from me, inside our gated, ultra-safe community, roughly

1000 feet from where I lived.

Keith, 24, was finishing medical school at UC Irvine and due to graduate in December. His attractive wife of only three months was a pediatric nurse, about three years older than Keith. Apparently, an intruder surprised them late at night, probably carrying a weapon that intimidated them into compliance. Investigators sketched out the likely scenario that Patti was directed to tie up Keith first, using brown macramé cord. He had Keith lie face-down on the couple's bed and placed a stack of dinner plates on his back. If the intruder heard the dishes fall and break, it would alert him to respond to Keith.

Then the assailant took Patti into an adjoining bedroom and raped her.

After the sexual assault, he brought Patti back to the couple's bedroom and had them both lying on their stomachs on the bed, with hands tied behind their backs. With one massive blow to the head, he killed Keith, which caused Patti to let out a blood-curdling scream, heard by one of the neighbors.

There were multiple blows to Patti's head, beyond reason, as if he hated women, which was likely. The weapon the perpetrator used to bludgeon them was never found, but a piece of brass was found embedded in Patti's skull, which led to the theory that he used materials from an outdoor sprinkler project in the works outside their home. While there was not much blood around Keith, Patti bled profusely from her wounds, evidencing the ferocity and hatred driving the killer.

The killings happened on a Tuesday night. Keith's father had been invited to dinner on the following Thursday, arrived promptly at 6:30 on that night, not realizing anything was amiss.

"I was surprised the door was locked," he recalled later. He found a key hidden near the door and let himself in. "When I walked in I thought the kids were off somewhere." He looked in the garage and both cars were there. "The door to the master bedroom was open. The door to the guest room, the room Keith and Patti used, was closed."

He opened the door tentatively, glanced in, and closed the door quickly. At first, he didn't think anything was amiss because the bed was completely made.

But something didn't seem right. "I opened the door again, and it was obvious there were bodies underneath the bedspread. So I pulled down the bedspread on the side close to the door, and Keith was there lying on his stomach with his head turned to the left, and he was all purple and had obviously been dead for a couple of days. I pulled down the bedspread on the other side, and Patti was lying on her stomach and looking in the same direction as Keith was. They were both laid out perfectly. The only difference between the two was that Patti was a bloody mess; the pillow was a mess bloodwise. I put the bedspread back up around their heads."

The horrific nature of the murders offended the peaceful, sheltered sense of security that permeated our upscale beach community. It couldn't be a random crime, I reasoned. It had to be either a lover's triangle committed by a spurned lover or a drug deal that went bad.

For the first time, I started locking the door to my townhouse.

* * * * * * *

CHAPTER FORTY-FOUR

THE NOT-SO-GREAT DEBATES

The first Presidential debate came around in late September, and Carter refused to attend, correctly believing that a good showing by Anderson would pull support primarily from him. Held in Baltimore, each candidate was given six questions to answer within two and a half minutes, followed by a rebuttal that could last a minute and a half.

Bill Moyers, LBJ's former press secretary, now at PBS, moderated the debate. Moyers had sometimes been accused of leftwing bias. It was said he earned his liberal bona fides by approving the infamous "Daisy Ad" showing a three-year-old girl in a field picking petals off daisies juxtaposed against a nuclear bomb's mushroom cloud. The fear-based emotional wallop from the ad helped LBJ defeat Barry Goldwater.

The other panelists on the stage included Carol Loomis from *Fortune Magazine*, syndicated columnist Daniel Greenburg, Charles Corddry from the *Baltimore Sun*, Lee May of the *L.A. Times*, Jane Bryant Quinn of *Newsweek*, and Soma Golden of the *New York Times*.

Anderson started off by stating his opposition to tax cuts, which Reagan (and almost every Republican) favored. He said the irresponsibility of an $11 billion tax cut could lead to a $60 billion deficit. He went on to propose something wildly unpopular, plopping a fifty-cent a gallon tax on gasoline, which could only hurt Joe Six-Pack.

As the debate wore on, I quickly realized I had underestimated the former movie actor. Anderson was somewhat bookish and talked about "incipient signs of renewed inflation," driven partly by gasoline jumping from $.80 a gallon to $1.30, with most of the proceeds enriching OPEC oil producers in the Middle East.

"Politicians should never use the word *incipient*," I whispered to one of our staffers as we watched at a debate party. Anderson's great mind and Phi Beta Kappa vocabulary caused him to fall into the Adlai Stevenson trap, allowing one's intellectual bent to set themselves apart from the common man.

Promoting more strict conservation by consumers, Anderson cited studies that the world supply of natural gas would completely run out by 2007 and oil supplies by 2027.

Then Reagan responded: "In 1920, (they) told us we only had enough oil left for 13 years, and 19 years later, told us we only had enough left for another 15 years. I think we are proving that we can go forward with conservation and benefit from that. But also, I think it is safe to say that we do have sources of energy that have not yet been used or found."

Anderson accused Reagan of doubling spending during the time he was governor of California, a stinging jab that potentially could undermine his supposed conservative credentials.

"Well, some people look up figures, and some people make up figures," Reagan replied in his folksy manner. "And John has just made up some very interesting figures ... The truth of the matter is, we did cut the increase in spending in half. We reduced, in proportion to other states, the per capita spending. We only increased the size of Government one-twelfth what it had increased in the preceding eight years. And one journal, the *San Francisco Chronicle*, said there was no question about the fact that Governor Reagan had prevented the State of California from going bankrupt."

My heart sank as he dodged the saber swung by Anderson. He seemed

CHAPTER FORTY-FOUR — THE NOT-SO-GREAT DEBATES

to have been well prepped and ready to answer any of our candidate's thrusts.

The last question of the evening came from Soma Golden who threw the equivalent of an incendiary device into the hall by bringing up the Catholic Church's warning to parishioners in Boston that it is sinful to vote for candidates who favor abortion.

This should be interesting, I thought, knowing Reagan had signed one of the most liberal abortion laws in the State of California, yet now seemed to have changed his tune in an attempt to woo the favor of Christian conservatives.

Reagan proceeded to duck the question and talked vaguely about the importance of returning to our spiritual roots. "Now, whether it is rightful, on a single issue, for anyone to advocate that someone should not be elected or not, I won't take a position on that."

Golden dug in her heels and repeated the question, unwilling to accept Reagan's artful ambiguity. "Okay ... I'll repeat my question. Do you approve the Church's action this week in Boston, and should a President be guided by organized religion on issues like abortion, equal rights, and defense spending?"

Anderson jumped into the fray with a bold response. "Ms. Golden, certainly the church has the right to take a position on moral issues. But to try, as occurred in the case that you mentioned, to try to tell the parishioners of any church, of any denomination, how they should vote, or for whom they should vote, I think violates the principle of separation of church and state. Now, Governor Reagan is running on a platform that calls for a Constitutional amendment banning abortion. I think that is a moral issue that ought to be left to the freedom of conscience of the individual. And for the state to interfere with a Constitutional amendment, and tell a woman that she must carry that pregnancy to term, regardless of her personal belief, that, I think, violates freedom of conscience as much as anything that I can think of."

"Yes! Yes! Yes!" I cried out at our debate party, as we all stood up and applauded Anderson.

Then Reagan gave a mealy-mouthed response to Golden's prodding. "The litmus test that John says is in the Republican platform, says no more than the judges to be appointed should have a respect for innocent life. Now, I don't think that's a bad idea. I think all of us should have a respect for innocent life.

"With regard to the freedom of the individual for choice with regard to abortion, there's one individual who's not being considered at all. That's the one who is being aborted. And I've noticed that everybody that is for abortion has already been born. I know this is a difficult and an emotional problem, and many people sincerely feel, on both sides of this, but I do believe that maybe we could find the answer through medical evidence, if we would determine once and for all, is an unborn child a human being? I happen to believe it is."

As an ardent believer in abortion, I couldn't abide Reagan's rejoinder, especially since he was a big hypocrite after signing a liberal abortion law. One couldn't help but think about Reagan's background, which included a divorce and fractured family.

In Reagan's three minutes for closing remarks, he said, "I've always believed that this land was placed here between the two great oceans by some divine plan. That it was placed here to be found by a special kind of people, people who had a special love for freedom and who had the courage to uproot themselves and leave hearth and homeland, and came to what, in the beginning, was the most undeveloped wilderness possible.

"We came from 100 different corners of the earth. We spoke a multitude of tongues. We landed on this Eastern shore and then went out over the mountains and the prairies and the deserts and the far western mountains to the Pacific, building cities and towns. We built a new breed of human called *an American*, a proud, an independent, and a most compassionate individual, for the most part.

"Two hundred years ago, Tom Paine, when the 13 tiny colonies were trying to become a nation, said we have it in our power to begin the world over again. Today, we're confronted with the horrendous problems that we've discussed here tonight. And some people in high positions of leadership tell us that the answer is to retreat. That the best is over. That we must cut back. That we must share in an ever-increasing scarcity.

"That we must, in the failure to be able to protect our national security as it is today, we must not be provocative to any possible adversary. Well, we, the living Americans, have gone through four wars. We've gone through a Great Depression in our lifetime that literally was worldwide and almost brought us to our knees. But we came through all of those things, and we achieved even new heights and new greatness. The living Americans today have fought harder, paid a higher price for freedom, and done more to advance the dignity of man than any people who ever lived on this earth. For 200 years, we've lived in the future, believing that tomorrow would be better than today. I believe the people of this country can, and together, we can begin the world over again. We can meet our destiny, and that destiny is to build a land here that will be, for all mankind, a shining city on a hill."

That phrase, "a shining city on a hill," seemed to resonate. His rhetoric was uplifting, but I was certain Anderson would rise to the moment we had all been waiting for.

In his closing, Anderson said, "A great historian, Henry Steele Commager, said that in their lust for victory, neither traditional party is looking beyond November. And he went on to cite three issues that their platforms totally ignore: atomic warfare, Presidential Directive 59 notwithstanding ...

What is Presidential Directive 59? I wondered.

"If we don't resolve that issue, all others become irrelevant. The issue of our natural resources; the right of posterity to inherit the earth, and what kind of earth will it be? The issue of nationalism, the recognition, he says, that every major problem confronting us is global, and cannot be solved by nationalism here or elsewhere, that is chauvinistic, that is parochial, that is as anachronistic as states' rights was in the days of Jefferson Davis. Those are some of the great issues—atomic warfare, the use of our natural resources, and the issue of nationalism—that I intend to be talking about in the remaining six weeks of this campaign, and I dare hope that the American people will be listening and that they will see that an Independent government of John Anderson and Patrick Lucey can give us the kind of coalition government that we need in 1980 to begin to solve our problems. Thank you."

My heart sank. Instead of soaring rhetoric that uplifted the mind and tugged at the heart, Anderson's close was clunky and filled with themes the typical American didn't really care about. The average patriotic, flag-waving union member doesn't see nationalism as chauvinistic or think it's one of the greatest problems confronting us.

In the week that followed, the bounce in the polls we hoped for failed to materialize. Unless something dramatic changed, Anderson could only be a spoiler candidate, the worst possible scenario. In October, more bad news arrived: Anderson would not be invited to the second and final debate, which ended up being watched by 80 million Americans, the most in history.

As a consolation, Ted Turner's fledgling news outlet, CNN, set up a pseudo-debate for Anderson at another location. Daniel Schorr, the first broadcast journalist hired by CNN, read the same questions to Anderson fielded by Reagan and Carter, but the tape-delayed experiment, beset with technical difficulties, didn't really work. It only highlighted our candidate as the absent also-ran.

On election night, I was in my car headed to the South Coast Plaza Hotel, when NBC news projected that Reagan had won in a landslide, based on their exit polling. What the hell? It was only 5:15 p.m. in California, and we still had nearly three hours before the polls closed. If we were not demoralized already, the news completely deflated our volunteers and their get-out-the-vote effort.

I met Barry VanFleet at the hotel, which was a gathering spot mostly for Republicans in Orange County. As we milled around in the foyer, I noticed a tall, distinguished gentleman in his 70s wearing a baggy gray suit that was probably stylish in the Fifties. As he bent forward to greet people he flashed a huge smile and projected a charisma beyond most politicians on the local or national scene.

CHAPTER FORTY-FOUR   THE NOT-SO-GREAT DEBATES

It was James Roosevelt, the eldest son of FDR, who *Time* once called the "Assistant President of the United States" when he served his father in the White House after Louis Howe died. He seemed to be a magnet for attracting controversy, however, and was forced to leave the White House in 1938 after he was accused of enriching himself on the side by guiding profitable contracts to his insurance company.

Roosevelt burnished his standing by serving with distinction in an elite combat unit of the Marines during WWII called Carlson's Raiders, earning the Silver Star and Navy Cross for his heroism at Makin Atoll and the Gilbert Islands in 1943. According to the citation that came with his medals, Roosevelt "voluntarily sought out the scenes of the heaviest fighting … continually accompanied the leading elements of the assault, exposing himself to constant danger. He "exposed himself to intense machine-gun and sniper fire," and later, "during evacuation, he displayed exemplary courage in personally rescuing three men from drowning in heavy surf."

After his valorous exploits in war, he continued in the insurance business and ran for governor of California against Earl Warren, but lost by 30 points. He ended up serving five terms as a Congressman from the 26th district, which is heavily democratic.

After Congress, he became an executive in Investors Overseas Service (IOS), based in Switzerland, which was run by Bernie Cornfeld and later, the notorious financier, Robert Vesco. Vesco embezzled $200 million from IOS, and Roosevelt's connection with him muddied his reputation once more and resulted in a Swiss arrest warrant. As IOS imploded, Roosevelt's third wife stabbed him with one of his war souvenirs, a marine combat knife, which ended the marriage and added another "dark chapter" to his life.

Somehow the lifelong democrat was able to extricate himself from his legal mess by moving back to California and associating himself with Richard Nixon, taking an active role in Democrats for Nixon as he worked toward Nixon's reelection in 1972. In the current election, he was for Reagan, which would have infuriated his parents.

We went over to say hello to him. "I'm a big admirer of your parents," I ventured, probably a minority opinion among the diehard Republicans crowding into the hotel that night. "In fact, I just finished reading *Eleanor and Franklin* by Joseph P. Lash." Lash, a personal friend to Mrs. Roosevelt, had access to her private papers at Hyde Park for his poignant account.

"I like Lash's treatment," Roosevelt said, "but you'll have to take a look at the book I wrote about them called *My Parents*." Roosevelt said he liked to see young people like ourselves engaged in public service and encouraged us to stay involved.

It went on to be a tough night for us Anderson supporters, with him getting only six percent of the vote nationally and failing to carry a single state. Carter conceded defeat relatively early, at 9:50 p.m. EST, having lost the popular vote by 10 points and by a crimson tidal wave in the Electoral College. His loss was the worst since Herbert Hoover's thrashing by FDR in 1932.

My youthful idealism about the prospects for an independent presidential candidacy suddenly seemed foolish. If Teddy Roosevelt hadn't been able to pull it off in 1912 when he bolted the Republican Party and ran as a "Bull Moose" Progressive, why had I been so naïve as to think Anderson would succeed?

My political distractions cost me dearly in my real estate job, which I put on the back burner for at least six months during the campaign. I got a phone call at Ashwill-Burke's office from the representative of an L.A. developer asking me for an update on one of their listings, a large commercial center near the Lake Forest off-ramp and the freeway.

What's going on there?" he demanded to know.

It was obvious from my response that I didn't have a clue. My partner on the listing pulled me aside the next day and delivered the news: "They want you off the listing," he informed, with a tone of sadness. I knew I had blown it and let them and my partner down because of my inactivity.

Then I faced a lecture from my manager. He said they were impressed with my potential (he even complimented my tennis game), but they

CHAPTER FORTY-FOUR — THE NOT-SO-GREAT DEBATES

needed to see more listings and more production in the form of closed sales and leases. I told him I would redouble my efforts, but inwardly, I was questioning myself. After only two years in real estate, I was already distracted and bored. My father's meteoric rise and success in real estate suddenly seemed more daunting than I had imagined. I began to wonder if I should reconsider my desire to follow in his footsteps.

I drove home, grabbed a beer, and went outside to watch the tail end of a sunset, with a few pale colors still dabbled across the beckoning night sky.

* * * * * * *

CHAPTER FORTY-FIVE

BECOMING AN ARTIST

I had dabbled with pen and ink drawings since high school, but I got inspired by a local artist named John Botz to pick up a brush and try my hand at painting. My mother bought one of his prints featuring a bouquet of flowers in a vase, sitting on a ledge looking toward a windswept ocean and Laguna coastal hills bursting with the colors of spring. She told me about his small gallery on Coast Highway in Laguna, so I dropped in one day.

Botz grew up in Washington, D.C., and later attended the Wharton School in Pennsylvania. After some time in the Navy, he became a buyer for I. Magnin in San Francisco. He lived in Paris for a while and also worked at the American Embassy in London, before he moved back to the U.S. and resumed his career in retail.

But on the side, he nurtured an interest in painting, working primarily in gouache. His first one-man show at the Pantechnicon in San Francisco was highly successful, with 32 of his 34 paintings sold on opening day. As his career advanced, Brunschwig and Fils commissioned him to design fabrics, along with Brule and Cie, and Pierre Frey of Paris.

When I walked in, he was sitting down in his gallery and the last pale gleam of afternoon light trickled through some large storefront windows.

"I'm so excited about your art," I exclaimed when we met.

"Thank you," he said. He appeared to be in his late 50s, with a slight build, longish stringy white hair, a bit like Warhol, and blotches on his skin that indicated he might not be well. "Matisse has been an influence. You would probably like his work."

"Oh, yes," I said, not wanting to admit I knew nothing about Matisse. Like most Americans, I was woefully ignorant about art history or contemporary art. "I've been doing some pen and ink drawings and would like to start painting," I continued. "Can you give me any advice."

"I like acrylics because they are so easy to use," he said. He pulled out a large brush with round bristles at the end. "I like to trim down the bristles so they're stubby at the end," he explained.

Following his lead, I bought myself a set of Liquitex acrylics, some brushes, and set myself up in the backyard, painting my garden. My first attempt was not very promising, but I continued, emulating the style of Botz. I even went to his framer and used white frames like his. At Christmas, I gave my parents one of my paintings, which produced a huge response.

Getting carried away with my new passion, I rented a small gallery space for $300 a month across the street from the Surf and Sand Hotel in Laguna Beach. I figured if I could sell one painting a month I would be able to pay the rent. It seemed like a no-brainer. Perhaps I was the one without brains because this became another distraction from my real estate career.

When I had everything set up, I invited all my friends and family to a gallery opening party, which included people from the tennis club and the Christian singles group. My sister told me later she overheard a group of girls speculating about who was going to snag me into marriage.

That night, I had no prospects whatsoever. My sister accused me of being too particular, which admittedly was true. I rarely dated someone more than once or twice if I perceived even a minor flaw in them. Influenced by the airbrushed beauties I saw in *Playboy* magazine,

I rejected women if their ankles were too thick, they were overweight, or their nose projected too far beyond the confines of their face.

My parents married young, 20- and 22-years-old. As time went on, Mom worried about the fact that I might reach the point of no return in bachelorhood, when a man becomes so set in his particularities and oddities that he might be unmarriageable.

Was I becoming an odd duck that fit my mother's description? I wondered.

To add fuel to her budding concerns, shortly after my foray into the art world, I dove into the realm of macrobiotics in a major way, a form of eating that grew out of my fascination with Eastern religion, a diet based on Yin and Yang principles.

Soon, I was eating lots of brown rice, Kukicha tea, tofu, and seaweed. Michio Kushi, a Japanese man who promoted macrobiotics in the U.S., became a big influence with his claims that the diet could prevent cancer and heart disease. Kushi and his wife cast a large shadow, founding Erewhon Natural Foods, the *East West Journal*, the Kushi Foundation, One Peaceful World, and the Kushi Institute, based in Brookline, Massachusetts.

One day, I was sitting in the art gallery with a young female employee. I typically hired young, attractive females to watch the gallery during the day and paid them the minimum wage, while I worked in real estate at my office in Irvine.

But this day, I happened to be there when a man walked into the gallery fuming. He began to yell and wave his arms around.

"How could you do this to John?" he shouted. "You've completely ripped him off, copying his style …"

It was John Botz's boyfriend, and he was not happy at the fact that I had so closely emulated his style. In my naiveté, driven by admiration for someone I viewed as a mentor, I shamelessly appropriated to a degree that had offended. I could only assume the man was sent over by Botz, and they shared the same grievance.

I was mortified and said very little. The high school girl sitting in the gallery was traumatized. "I hope you rot in hell!" he bellowed, as he stormed out.

* * * * * * *

After I turned 25, I decided I would leave real estate, go to law school, and pursue a career in the law with political aspirations. After I broke this news to Mom and Dad, they invited me to dinner and dropped an unexpected offer in my lap.

"I've always thought about you working with me at Ellis & Lane," Dad began. He proceeded to make an offer that was difficult for me to refuse, to join him in business, with me starting a new division that would be involved in brokerage of investment properties.

Even though I found real estate tedious, the prospect of working alongside my father appealed to an unfulfilled yearning for a closer connection to a man I admired deeply, but knew on only a shallow level. Casting aside internal doubts about my passion for the real estate business, I joined the family firm, nurturing hopes of finding two things that were elusive: success in the business world and paternal love.

* * * * * * *

CHAPTER FORTY-SIX

HUNTING FOR A WIFE

My Salt Company friend, Dixie Spratt, set me up with one of her friends, Missy Welbourne. They grew up in Pasadena together, were in the same sorority at USC, and had remained good friends after college.

"Missy is president of the Spinsters," Dixie informed me. I had never heard of the Spinsters Club and wasn't sure being president of such a group would be a good harbinger.

Founded in 1926 as a sister organization to the Bachelors, they were known for their annual Spinsters Ball, often held at the Biltmore Hotel, an aging dowager in downtown L.A., which seemed to fit the bill. Mary Lou Loper of the *L.A. Times* captured the flavor of one of their balls:

"The Spinsters Mardi Gras Masquerade Ball was receiving rave A-pluses from its 600 guests. That was early in the evening during the pre-cocktail parties in private suites at the Biltmore Hotel and during the exotic cocktail party in the renovated Rendezvous Court, the Biltmore's old lobby. The mood held until 2:30 a.m. That's when Jim Fox and His Orchestra collapsed, and the exuberant yuppies went home."

The term yuppie described a demographic of young, upwardly-mobile professionals known for their preppy style, who might have had yuppie sympathies in the late Sixties, but traded their torn jeans and radicalism for a career in business, law, Wall Street, or the halls of Congress. Often they were socially liberal and fiscally conservative. Although I wasn't fond of the label, it seemed to capture my drift in moving from Berkeley to Orange County.

I picked Missy up at her modest, airy, walk-up apartment in Hollywood that appeared to have been built in the 1940s or '50s. She was tall, slender, and looked athletic. Dixie said she was an outstanding golfer and tennis player. She had a wholesome attractiveness that suggested she could have played Katherine Hepburn's sister or sidekick in a classic movie.

We drove to the Cinerama Dome on Sunset Boulevard near Vine, the iconic, white geodesic concrete dome developed by Buckminster Fuller and French architect Pierre Cabrol. Years ago, I had seen *How the West was Won* in Cinerama on their 86-foot screen, a monumental experience for an eight-year-old.

As Missy and I stood in a long line to see the latest *Star Wars* film—an update on the Western I had seen there—a marvelous repartee developed between the two of us, with her quick-witted charm and glib tongue on rare display. The chemistry was nearly instantaneous, striking a note of voluble effervescence.

After the movie, we went to a small Italian restaurant on Little Santa Monica Boulevard in Beverly Hills, where waiters and patrons were often opera singers and would spontaneously break into song. I learned Missy was part of a light opera company performing Gilbert and Sullivan's *Madame Butterfly*, so after a few tenors got up to sing, I goaded Missy to join in the reverie. I was duly impressed when she stood and gave a rousing rendition of "I could have danced all night" from *My Fair Lady*.

On our second date, I drove up to see her perform in *Butterfly*. She had a minor part, and overall the production was colorful but boring to me, since I had little appreciation for opera, but I did my best to hide that fact.

CHAPTER FORTY-SIX

The relationship seemed to quickly turn serious, and she invited me to spend a golf and tennis weekend at her parents' townhouse in Pauma Valley, in eastern San Diego County. They were waspy, refined, solid citizens, the opposite of flashy or pretentious. Warm and welcoming to me, we soon discovered a crazy coincidence that we had been vacationing at the La Jolla Beach and Tennis Club during the last two weeks in August for the last decade.

A few weeks later, I invited Missy to spend the night at my place in Niguel Shores. When she arrived, I could tell she was nervous about staying with me. She seemed to be a more serious Christian than I was. In dating girls I met at the Christian singles group, I set a standard that there would be no intercourse, but I soon discovered there was varying degrees of "outer-course" going on in these circles.

I tried to make Missy feel more at ease, but another snag developed in my plans for romance. She started sneezing incessantly, her eyes got red and puffy, as if she was allergic to something in my house. I discovered she had a serious allergy to dust, and as a clueless bachelor, I had never vacuumed the shag carpet running through the house. I did some light cleaning of the bathroom occasionally, but didn't even own a vacuum cleaner or realize the importance of it. Now, I did, as our magical time turned misty for the wrong reasons.

My paternal grandmother's second husband, Vestal, had always told me that if I got serious about a woman, I should take her camping as the ultimate test of a relationship. So Missy and I went off to the local mountains together, but got hit by an unexpected rainstorm. There is nothing worse than camping in the rain, and both of us got a little testy as we dealt with the drenching. I suppose that was the point of grandpa's advice, to remove you from your comfort zone, and to inject a bit of hardship into a courtship to see how you both respond. We both were miserable under the circumstances, which I took as a bad omen for the future.

Even though Missy seemed to check almost every box on my list, I had two qualms. Our personalities had an amazing chemistry, and we were very much alike, but the closer we got to know each other, the more we began to relate to each other like a brother and sister who know how to push each other's buttons in the wrong way, with our keen wits sometimes wounding. Secondly, I didn't have a strong attraction to her physically, and I wondered to myself if that would matter in the long run. Would I stray in my affections? On some ideal plane of human existence, I would like to think I would remain loyal, but I wasn't sure I wanted to test the principle.

I broke up with her at probably the worst possible location: as our families vacationed together in La Jolla. We took a long walk on the beach after dinner, and I broke the news as gently as I could. She didn't take it well. "What about all the sex?" she blurted out, revealing that I had violated her Christian conscience in ways that I had been blind to and viewed as an acceptable compromise. Since we never had intercourse, I was shocked by her charge and didn't respond, but in her shock and hurt, I could tell she felt violated.

* * * * * * *

CHAPTER FORTY-SEVEN
RECLAIMING YOUTH

At 27, I settled into a comfortable, carefree bachelor lifestyle. On the weekends, I would catch the early morning surf at Salt Creek, then shower, change, and drive over to the tennis club in my BMW 528i to play doubles, then go to a local health food store to pick up a sandwich and take it down to the beach in the afternoon to read and work on my tan.

At the health food store, the girl behind the counter making the sandwiches was a knockout blonde named Karin, with flawless features. Her parents were Berkeley grads I had met in the local alumni group. I was smitten by her flashing blue eyes, attractive figure, and ready smile. She seemed to respond to my flirtations with an easy laugh. There was only one small hitch. She was 17, a graduating high school senior, with plans to attend UCLA.

I hired her to work in my art gallery toward the end of her senior year, but once she turned 18 in June and graduated, I pounced like a foolish letch chasing the fading dream of eternal youth. While nine years is not an insurmountable gap between a man and a woman at a more mature stage of life, it was pronounced at this stage. There was already surprising generational distance between us in her attitudes and tastes, especially in music.

She liked artists I had never heard of, but I decided to broaden my music taste and indulge her teenage fancies. For our first date, we drove to Westwood and had dinner at a restaurant called Yesterdays. She was decked out in a black leather skirt and heels. When we walked into the restaurant and she went to the restroom, a stranger turned to me and said, "You're one lucky guy." After dinner, we rode a pedi-cab to Dillon's, a three-story disco.

After our date, she sent me a poem:

"Poetic Injustice"

Marky was just Karin's boss,
That's all—or so it seemed.
Until that date to Westwood,
Marky never would have dreamed…

A normal date for dinner,
Dancing, champagne, beer,
A memory made for me that night,
The rest is history, dear …

Hidden Motivations (??),
No innuendos lost,
"Jacuzzi" is the code word for
the way to get your boss.

No Jacuzzi – try the bedroom
(We've pulled this one before)
Karin kisses wet and wild …
But that's what towels are for!

CHAPTER FORTY-SEVEN — RECLAIMING YOUTH

> Boss turned into more than boss
> A hybrid romance bloomed
> No chance now for normalcy
> Platonic-ness was doomed.
>
> Now life with me is lots of fun,
> There is no life without me,
> I know I'm "RAD", etcetera …
> You're lucky to have found me!
>
> So now what does the future hold,
> (Aside from spending money?)
> I must confess this sure is nice,
> See ya Sunday, honey!

On our second date over the Fourth of July weekend, we drove south to see Flock of Seagulls and The FIXX in San Diego. The concert was so loud my ears throbbed for two days. We stayed at my parents' oceanfront townhouse in Leucadia and made a "cultural" side trip to see the California mission at San Luis Rey.

She penned this note afterward:

Although the weather was less than perfect, the weekend was both fun and cultural. I'm sure that Madame Serra misses us now that we are gone, and I miss all of those gorgeous (!!) jarheads. Ah, yes, how can we forget the 4th? Saved by Zero … what does it mean?!

For our third date, we drove up to L.A. and had dinner at The Moustache Café, then over to the Wilshire Theater to see the Australian group INXS (in excess). Karin was wild about their lead singer, Michael Hutchence, and their album *Shabooh Shoobah*. I soon discovered why she responded to Hutchence, who dominated the relatively small venue with his charismatic stage persona and a voice and manner that reminded me of Jim Morrison of The Doors. It was as if the former rock legend had come back to life, reincarnated into the body of Hutchence.

Sparing no expense on this young lass, I completely lost my senses and put together the most expensive date of my life. First, we drove to a restaurant in Newport Beach near the airport for dinner. After dinner, I had arranged for a helicopter to take us from John Wayne Airport to the Santa Monica airport. But flying near LAX, the pilot apparently made a mistake, straying too close to a plane taking off, which caused him to take abrupt evasive action that was gut churning.

Was it worth dying to earn the affection of this young head-turner? I wondered.

At the small airport, I had a limo waiting to drive us to The Forum to see David Bowie's Serious Moonlight Tour, which followed his hit album, *Let's Dance.* Bowie was at the top of his game in the summer of 1983, and had taken a lead role in designing the sets, which included giant columns he called condoms, along with an enormous moon and a hand. Earl Slick was Bowie's lead guitarist that night after Stevie Ray Vaughn dropped out following a kerfuffle about a cocaine habit.

Afterward, a limo took us back to my car in Newport Beach, and I whisked her south to my townhouse after midnight, where we kissed, and I rubbed her back, but she got testy about going any further. After such a monumental evening, the romantic side of things seemed to dissolve into nothingness, which left me feeling empty, calling to mind Mick Jagger's famous line, "I can't get no satisfaction."

After pursuing the best the world has to offer, why do I still feel a gnawing, void inside myself, I wondered. *Is Karin in love with me or the things I can buy for her?*

She began to send me handwritten and typed notes of her free-floating thoughts that seemed to be the product of a brilliant but somewhat twisted mind. With a felt-tipped pen, she scrawled all sorts of colorful arrows, underlinings, diagrams, and even geometry problems. I slowly began to realize she was mentally unstable, particularly her obsession with Marilyn Monroe and a fantasy that I was JFK. (I did try my impression of his voice on her, and she loved it.)

Toward the end of the summer, we went to see Woody Allen's new mockumentary, *Zelig*, where Allen plays Leonard Zelig, a man with an identity crisis, who takes on the personality of those he is with. Zelig finally finds himself with the help of a psychiatrist played by Mia Farrow. Unfortunately, I drew some parallels between myself and Zelig's sad mental state, which seemed to be headed south due to my relationship with Karin.

My breakup with her was a nasty affair, with Karin telling me she never loved me and had only used me for my money, exactly what I had suspected but never wanted to fully acknowledge. It was stinging, however, to hear it coming from her own mouth, and even though splitting up was painful, I knew it was the best hope to restore my own fraying mental condition.

After our breakup, she sent me a shocking letter that explained a missing piece in my understanding of her:

Mark,

This is very hard to admit to anyone because it signifies finally that I am acknowledging a major problem, but I guess I cannot help myself in this ... I have proven that over and over again. I am bulimic, if you understand what that means. It is a horrible thing, but it is a psychological illness, and no doubt I am psychologically ill. I don't know what else to say. Please try not to judge me. Although I know it is hard not to.

This is a very delicate subject as you may well know. Please help me.

I had never heard of bulimia, and nursing my own wounds from our relationship felt like I was in no position to help her. Lacking compassion, I never responded to her letter, and we drifted away from each other as she went off to school.

* * * * * * *

CHAPTER FORTY-EIGHT
CHANCE MEETING AT ABRAMSON'S HOUSE

I was relieved knowing Karin left for UCLA in late August, and I wouldn't be running into her for a while. Nursing scars from that relationship, I made my way back to the Christian group, attending one of their Bible studies in Corona Del Mar, held at the home of Gerald Abramson, Jr.

Gerald was unusual. With a thin build and pale features, he was quite possibly the most socially awkward person I had ever encountered. He was also the son of the founder of a large savings and loan. A lonely child, his parents divorced when he was 10 years old. After the divorce, his father, Gerald, Sr., remarried a fashion consultant who had started her own modeling agency and served as an advisor for a TV show.

Gerald, Jr. was 18 when tragedy struck, and his father died while the family traveled together in Europe. An only child, Gerald inherited a vast fortune and a gold-plated name associated with his father's philanthropy in Los Angeles, while his stepmom went to live in the penthouse suite at the Beverly Wilshire Hotel in Beverly Hills.

To add complexity to Gerald's personal situation, he had a condition known as Tourette Syndrome, so that during conversations, Gerald manifested unusual tics such as pronounced eye blinking, sniffing, and erratic facial movements. He had also embraced the teachings of a Calvinist theologian, R.J. Rushdoony, father of a movement that wanted to impose Old Testament laws on society.

That night, a guy named Dave was leading the study. Before he began his talk he said, "I just finished a book I want to recommend: *Evidence That Demands a Verdict*, by Josh McDowell." I filed the name away in my head, thinking it might be something I should read. After Dave finished his teaching, he had everybody in the room, about 25 young men and women, count off, one through five, so that we could break out into smaller discussion groups.

I landed in a group with a striking blonde named Sally, brought to the group that night by Dave Brandenberg, Dixie Spratt's former paramour. I learned later that Sally was starting an art career and had moved to Laguna Beach, where she was juried into the Festival of Arts. Sitting at her booth, Brandenberg happened to walk by, and they immediately recognized one another from attending high school together in Evergreen, Colorado.

During the conversation, Brandenberg invited her to attend the singles' Bible study and said he knew an artist in the group, Mark Ellis.

My first thought when I talked to Sally at the end of the small group discussion was, *Oh, no. I don't need another blonde in my life.* As we chatted briefly, I sensed she was a sincere Christian because the love of Jesus seemed to transmit through her eyes.

As I left the study that night, Sally was talking with Don Wilson, a handsome and successful guy that worked with Segerstrom, the owner of South Coast Plaza, a hugely successful shopping destination. I could tell that Don had zeroed in on Sally and would probably be the one to land a date with her.

I called Dave Brandenberg the next day to get Sally's phone number. "She told me not to give it out," he said. That was disappointing news, and I didn't make any further attempt to pursue her for several weeks.

After two months went by, I called Brandenberg again to ask for Sally's number. I'm not sure if he thought I was being a pest or merely

CHAPTER FORTY-EIGHT — CHANCE MEETING AT ABRAMSON'S HOUSE

persistent, but he grudgingly acceded to my request. "Okay, okay, I'll give you her number, but don't tell her where you got it," he cautioned.

I called Sally and established our mutual interest in art as a pretext for a lunch date. I chose my favorite restaurant in Laguna, The Place Across the Street from the Laguna Hotel, and arrived first, wearing business attire: dark brown slacks, a powder blue oxford button-down shirt, and a brown tie. I had a *Time Magazine* in tow in case she didn't show up.

Thankfully, she did arrive, and we sat on the outdoor deck overlooking the cars streaming by on Pacific Coast Highway, within sight of waves lapping against Main Beach a block away. Sally had a dazzlingly beautiful face and wore her hair like Princess Diana. In fact, she bore a striking resemblance to the British royal.

We seemed to hit it off and toward the end of the lunch, I casually mentioned that I would be getting together that night, October 11th, to celebrate my mother's birthday.

"Oh, today's my birthday, too!" she exclaimed. It seemed like an unusual coincidence, that our first date would be on their shared birthdays. I took it as a hopeful sign. Over the course of the next week, we had several dates and seemed to laugh much of the time, another good sign.

But then she dropped something unexpected on me. "I'm leaving for Guam to visit a friend," she told me, explaining that her friend Jan was married to a pilot based in Guam, doing aerial reconnaissance for the military. During his lengthy missions, she had become the lonely military wife and invited Sally for some much-needed woman-to-woman time.

"I'll only be gone a month," she said breezily, which I figured I could live with. Before she left, I sent a big bouquet of flowers to the small apartment she shared with a lesbian on Y Place, behind the fire station in Laguna.

After a month came and went and Thanksgiving rolled around, I called her apartment. Her roommate said Sally had decided to stay longer. Then I came up with a brainstorm.

I'll record a Christmas greeting on a cassette tape and send it to her in hopes she won't forget me.

I decided to have some fun with my little project and used impersonated voices and music in the background in an attempt to get her attention and create a lasting impression. Jimmy Stewart was my best impersonation, so I had him introducing various celebrities and public figures, all wishing Sally a Merry Christmas.

More weeks went by, and I never heard anything from her. *I guess my attempt at humor bombed,* I thought. After weeks turned into months, I began to forget about Sally and turned my attention elsewhere.

* * * * * * *

CHAPTER FORTY-NINE

RECKONINGS

One day, I was tooling around in my 528i with rabbit fur seat covers when I spied a Christian bookstore. It was a bright sunny day. There was a brightness in the car reminiscent of the car ride with my real estate broker, Shep Daniels, when he invited me to attend the Christian singles group. Inexplicably, the light seemed to impel my heart to turn into the parking lot where the bookstore was located.

I remembered the name of the book the Bible study leader had recommended. I went into the store and purchased a copy of *Evidence That Demands a Verdict*. I was put off by the book cover, which featured a courtroom gavel coming down on a wooden cross. The sight of the cross offended me on a subconscious level I couldn't understand. On a hill above Pacific Coast Highway near my house, a church had erected a large white cross they lit up at night. When I was going off to party on a Friday or Saturday night, the sight of that lighted cross provoked ill feelings, and I usually averted my gaze. Why did the sight of a cross trigger such disquiet in me?

I had to admit that after spending seven years in the Christian group, I didn't really know what I believed. I believed in God to some extent, but my thoughts about God were also influenced by Ram Dass and his Eastern philosophy. I thought that all pathways lead to God, and there must be some way to find unity between the various faiths and isms.

Do I really believe in the God of the Bible? I wondered. *What about Jesus?* At 29 years old, I figured it was time to settle these questions. Because of my rationalistic bent, I couldn't make a blind leap of faith. I needed something more solid and thought that, perhaps, *Evidence* might be the book to help me form some conclusions.

I began to read the book at night, sitting alone in the corner of my dark-paneled bedroom with shag carpeting. There were two chapters that seemed critical to me. One examined the way the Bible was put together. *Had it been changed? Could I trust it as a source for ultimate truth?* McDowell describes the science of studying ancient manuscripts to determine their authenticity. With over 5,000 ancient Greek manuscripts in various forms that could be compared with one another, and thousands more in other languages from the Mediterranean region, McDowell made the case that there was more solid evidence for the authenticity of the Bible than any other single book from antiquity.

The fact that it was written before the printing press was a key for me. For some nefarious and powerful cabal to change the Bible would have required them to also change the thousands of manuscript copies, which all bore witness to the essential doctrines of the Christian faith. That seemed impossible to me.

Resolving my trust issues about the underlying manuscripts, I knew the chapter about the resurrection of Jesus would be the most critical. *If Jesus really died on the cross and was raised bodily from the dead several days later, that set him apart from Buddha and Muhammad and every other religious figure,* I reasoned.

I began chapter 10, "The Resurrection – Hoax or History," with mounting anticipation. The author quoted a German theologian, Wolfhart Pannenberg, stating, "Whether the resurrection of Jesus took place or not is a historical question, and the historical question at this point has to be decided on the basis of historical argument." I had always loved history, and a historical argument made sense to me.

McDowell lays out various facts that may be known about the manner of Roman crucifixion, burial practices in ancient Israel, rock-hewn tombs in and around Jerusalem, the stone rolled in front of the entrance to the tomb, and the seal placed on the tomb by a Roman guard that watched over the tomb at the command of Roman Governor Pontius Pilate, who served under Tiberius.

Then the author examines the various theories proposed by critics over the years to explain away the resurrection.

First, the idea that Jesus never actually died on the cross, but merely swooned, and later revived in the tomb. But to believe this, one would have to believe the Roman soldiers were fooled about Jesus' death as well as Joseph and Nicodemus, who prepared his body for burial. Since the body of Jesus was wrapped like a mummy with yards of grave clothes, weighted down with spices, he would have to somehow extricate himself from the tightly wound wrappings, roll away the heavy stone covering the entrance, get past the Roman guards, and walk miles on wounded feet. Such a scenario seemed highly improbable to me.

McDowell also examines the theory that the disciples stole the body, an idea floated from the beginning by the religious authorities. As E.F. Kenan noted in the book, "The enemies of Jesus had no motive for removing his body; the friends of Jesus had no power to do so."

Le Camus puts it this way: "If Jesus, who had been laid in the tomb on Friday, was not there on Sunday, either he was removed, or he came forth by his own power. There is no other alternative."

At the time of the crucifixion, the disciples were a cowardly lot who fled during his trial. They had neither the courage nor the physical power to go up against the soldiers guarding the tomb. Could all the Roman soldiers have been asleep at the same time, while the disciples crept in, moved the large stone covering the entrance, stole the body, and carried it out with not one soldier being awakened? It seemed unlikely.

And since all the early church leaders were martyred for their faith, would they have gone to their death to support a lie? I wondered.

When the disciples first saw the empty tomb, they were astounded by the condition of the grave clothes, which were still neatly wound around each other, as if the body of Jesus had mysteriously passed through them. "The grave clothes give a silent testimony to the impossibility of theft." As Merrill Tenney noted: "No robbers would have rewound the wrappings in their original shape, for there would not have been time to do so. They would have flung the clothes down in disorder and fled with the body."

Could the disciples have gone to the wrong tomb? The author makes the point that "… if the women went to the wrong tomb (an empty sepulcher), then the Sanhedrin (governing Jewish authorities) could have gone to the right tomb and produced the body (if Jesus did not rise). This would have shut the disciples up forever!"

Another theory that floated over the years is that the post-resurrection appearances of Jesus were merely hallucinations. But hallucinations are particular to certain kinds of people, with a certain psychological makeup that predisposes them to hallucinations. One would have to believe that the manifestations of Jesus to His disciples in smaller and larger groups, and in His appearances with crowds as large as 500, everyone suffered delusions simultaneously. This also seems implausible.

Jesus told Thomas before He died: "I am the way and the truth and the life. No one comes to the Father except through me" (John 14:6). Ram Dass had tried to explain away this verse, but its powerful implications for the exclusivity of Jesus as a singular religious figure gnawed at me.

Later, the disciple Thomas doubted that Jesus had actually risen from the dead. He said, "Unless I see the nail marks in his hands and put my finger where the nails were, and put my hand into his side, I will not believe" (John 20:25).

The Scripture continues: "A week later, His disciples were in the house again, and Thomas was with them.

"Though the doors were locked, Jesus came and stood among them and said, 'Peace be with you!' Then he said to Thomas, 'Put your finger here; see my hands. Reach out your hand and put it into my side. Stop doubting and believe.'

CHAPTER FORTY-NINE — RECKONINGS

Thomas said to him, "My Lord and my God!"

Then Jesus told him, "Because you have seen me, you have believed; blessed are those who have not seen and yet have believed" (John 20:26-29).

McDowell concludes his chapter by stating: "He is risen, He is risen indeed."

When I finished the chapter about the resurrection, I did not need any further convincing. I had arrived at a point where I could see that I had not done such a great job of running my life. I had lived solely for an unholy trinity: me, myself, and I. Where did that get me at the end of the day? What if I let God take control?

I flipped to the end of McDowell's book, where he presents the Four Spiritual Laws as an appendix. I had seen this presentation in little tracts handed out by Jesus freaks and resisted it previously. But now I considered its message.

I could see that I was a sinful person. "For all have sinned and fall short of the glory of God" (Romans 3:23).

I had been a rebel, running from God, which left me separated from Him. "For the wages of sin is death ..." (Romans 6:23) What I earned by sinning was a farther and farther distance from God, a deadening of my soul to the things of God that would ultimately result in my physical death and eternal separation from God in hell.

But God saw my sinful, separated condition and kept loving me, wooing my heart, pursuing relationship with me. "But God demonstrates his own love for us in this: while we were still sinners, Christ died for us" (Romans 5:8).

McDowell displays a little diagram showing a holy God separated from sinful man, a chasm between the two, with the cross of Jesus in the middle, connecting them. "This diagram illustrates that God has bridged the gulf which separates us from Him by sending His Son, Jesus Christ, to die on the cross in our place to pay the penalty for our sins."

Law Four states that we must "individually receive Jesus Christ as Savior and Lord. Then we can know and experience God's love and plan for our lives." When someone offers you a gift, what do you do? You receive it and open the gift. "But as many as received Him, to them He gave the right to become children of God, to those who believe in His name" (John 1:12 NKJV).

I could see there was nothing I could do to work my way to heaven by being a "good enough person." I could never meet God's perfect, holy standard. Alternatively, I could accept the free gift He offered me, a remarkable bargain. "For by grace you have been saved through faith, and that not of yourselves; it is the gift of God, not of works, lest anyone should boast" (Ephesians 2:8-9 NKJV).

The author goes on to say, "Receiving Christ involves turning to God from self, (repentance) and trusting Christ to come into our lives, to forgive our sins, and to make us the kind of people He wants us to be. Just to agree intellectually that Jesus Christ is the Son of God and that He died on the cross for our sins is not enough. Nor is it enough to have an emotional experience. We receive Jesus Christ by faith, as an act of the will."

Then the author displays two circular diagrams, one showing a self-directed life, with self on the throne and Jesus outside the life. The second circle shows Christ in the life and on the throne, with the self yielding to Jesus, resulting in harmony with God's plan.

I could readily see that I had been on the throne of my life, wanting to be the captain of my own ship, running my life my way. But living for self had been empty at the end of the day, and I was ready for change, ready to live for someone higher and greater than myself.

"YOU CAN RECEIVE CHRIST RIGHT NOW THROUGH PRAYER," the text stated in bold letters that shouted at me.

I dropped to my knees on the shag carpet and prayed the prayer that McDowell had printed in his book.

"Lord Jesus, I need you. Thank you for dying on the cross for my sins. I open the door of my life and receive You as my Savior and Lord. Thank you for forgiving my sins and giving me eternal life. Take control of the throne of my life. Make me the kind of person You want me to be."

CHAPTER FIFTY

PALM SPRINGS RENDEZVOUS

A couple of months later, I learned that one of my fraternity brother's former girlfriends, Laurie Fiorina, was flying down to Palm Springs with a group of friends. I was attracted to her, so I let her know I would be out there staying at my parents' condo at the same time.

I drove out to the desert resort with hopeful expectations, but over the course of the weekend, I could not find any time to be alone with Laurie. Nothing seemed to go right in our interactions. Previously, I thought there had been some potential sparks between the two of us, but they seemed to have vanished like an oasis in the desert sands.

On Sunday afternoon, I offered to drive her to Palm Springs airport for her flight back to the Bay Area. *At last, this will be my chance to see if there's any chemistry between us,* I thought.

As I walked her from the parking lot toward the terminal, I saw Edwin Camp, a friend of Dixie Spratt's, standing on the curb by himself, looking in our direction, as if he was waiting for someone. Tall, sturdy, and handsome, Camp came from a prominent farming family in Bakersfield.

"Edwin! It's great to see you. What are you doing here?" I asked cheerily.

"I'm flying up to the Bay Area," he replied. I introduced him to Laurie, and the two of them hit it off immediately. It turned out they were on the same flight.

So I watched the two of them walk off together toward the plane, and I gave a halfhearted wave. They didn't bother to even turn around, they were so engrossed in conversation with one another.

By now, the sun had dropped low behind the mountain that forms a giant wall along the edge of Palm Springs. I got into my car and began the two-hour drive home. I could not have been more dispirited and dejected as I made my way down Weir Canyon on the 91 Freeway.

But in the darkness of the undeveloped canyon, someone had erected a lighted white cross on the hillside.

When I saw it, I cried out in desperation and despair, "God, I've been an utter failure finding a wife …" As a new Christian, I heard people talk about giving your problems to God and letting Him handle them. I began to pray with a fervency gushing up from my despondent state of mind:

"I give up, God. You take over. Please God, help me find a wife."

Forty-five minutes later, I walked into my townhouse on Moonsail in Niguel Shores. I went over to the answering machine and hit the play button. I almost fell over when I heard a familiar woman's voice say:

"Hi, this is Sally. I'm home from Asia, and I just wanted to say hi. It would be great to see you."

My heart leapt when I heard her voice. It was the greatest, and fastest, answer to prayer I could have hoped for or imagined.

Later, Sally revealed to me that when she returned from Asia, she played my cassette tape for her mother, Harriet, who had driven out from Colorado for a visit.

After she heard the tape, she asked, "Who is this guy?"

"Oh, it's just a guy I met," Sally replied.

"Did you ever thank him for the tape?"

"No," Sally replied sheepishly.

Then Harriet did something very uncharacteristic. She got very stern, slammed her fist on the kitchen table, and pointed her finger at Sally.

"You are looking for the wrong thing in a man! I want you to call this guy and thank him for the tape."

So Sally's mother was responsible for her phone call.

Within two weeks of seeing each other, I knew we would be married.

* * * * * * *

CHAPTER FIFTY-ONE

THE ASK

After a six-month whirlwind romance, I felt it was time to ask Sally to marry me. I had a six-month, fish-or-cut-bait rule when dating. I didn't want to waste anyone's time if things were not going in the right direction.

I went over to my parents' house and hinted around about the seriousness of my intentions toward Sally.

"Do you have an engagement ring?" Mom asked, clearly steering me in a direction.

"No," I replied. She retrieved a diamond ring that had been in the family. "You could use this to ask her," she ventured. Mom and Dad seemed to be enthusiastic about my intentions.

I planned the perfect evening. Sally and I would have dinner at the Chart House restaurant overlooking Dana Point Harbor. Then I would walk her out to a promontory with a spectacular view of the boats and the lights, and I would propose. At dinner, I kept the small container holding the ring hidden in the pocket of a red jacket.

After our meal, I walked Sally toward the overlook, but as we walked, she began to complain she had a headache and didn't feel well.

Oh, no, I thought. *I can't ask her to marry me when she feels awful.*

For the next week, I carried the ring around in the red jacket. I think Sally began to wonder about that jacket.

The following Saturday, I took her to Diz's As-Is, a uniquely Laguna restaurant with a 1940s décor, mismatching old plates, flowery French cloth wallpaper, and complimentary pâté de maison and vermouth when seated at your table.

After dinner we went back to Sally's apartment on Y Place and began to talk on the couch. She had checked out a book from the library about Sir Winston Churchill's life, with a section devoted to his 57-year marriage to Clementine. She knew I was a Churchill fan. After we perused some of the photos in the book of the remarkable couple and their enduring marriage, I dropped to my knees in front of Sally. She was still seated on the couch.

I reached out for her hand and held it with loving affection. Then I looked in her eyes and asked, "Will you spend the next 57 years with me?"

After she said yes, I reached into my red jacket and retrieved the little container I had carried around for a week, pulled out the ring, and presented it to her.

"I wondered why you were carrying that red jacket around all week!" she exclaimed. We laughed, and I fell asleep on her couch, completely exhausted.

* * * * * * *

CHAPTER FIFTY-TWO

WEDDING BELLS

We found a small, friendly church near Laguna Beach High School and a pastor to marry us. As we shopped together to assemble a gift list, we had our first major fight over the color of the pots for our kitchen. She liked pots that were fire-engine red, and I thought they looked garish.

I soon learned the time-honored and appropriate response of husbands in the face of such disagreements, which is to artfully cave and mutter, "Yes, dear."

We had a six-month engagement, and as a relatively new Christian, I had a budding awareness of the importance of maintaining purity before our wedding day. We were like crazed chipmunks around each other, but I felt a growing conviction that we should cool things down until the appointed day. So I proposed that we back away from the physical side of our relationship during the final month leading up to our marriage.

We borrowed a larger church in the heart of Laguna's village for the wedding, with about 150 people expected. An hour before the nuptials, the groomsmen took me for a drink at an ivy-covered restaurant at the end of Forest Avenue. Downing a drink before the momentous occasion seemed to be in keeping with the first miracle of Jesus, turning water into wine at the wedding feast in Cana.

When the groomsmen and I first entered the sanctuary with its high, cathedral-like arches, I was overcome with emotion and almost hyperventilated as I stood in the front, looking over the crowd. Mom looked at me with sudden alarm and mouthed, "Breathe ... breathe!" insistently.

I slowly began to inhale and exhale as I caught my first glimpse of Sally walking down the aisle with her father. What a beautiful bride God had given me, so much more than I had hoped for or imagined! She looked radiant as she seemed to glide toward me in slow motion. Nothing could compare to this pinnacle moment. My heart was overflowing with love and adoration for her, with Sally giving all of herself to me and me to her. It was overwhelming to think she trusted me with the gift of herself, all of herself, trusting that I would love and respect her all the days of our lives on this earth.

Pastor Jack filled the ceremony with scriptural references, providing an anchor of truth foundational to the meaning of marriage, an institution that originated in the mind of God. A family friend, operatic tenor Dennis McNeil, sang *The Lord's Prayer* in such a powerful way that I felt an electric charge run up and down my tux-covered torso.

Sally and I recited our vows to each other in the sight of God, the minister, and all of our guests. We then shared a prolonged kiss at the altar and were introduced for the first time as husband and wife to raucous cheers. With my heart full of love and joy, I escorted my new bride down the aisle.

After the photographer took our group photos, I escorted Sally to my dad's Mercedes. He chauffeured us to our reception at a restaurant near John Wayne Airport called Chanteclair where we had planned a very elegant lunch menu. After visiting with our guests and eating a few bites of the meal, we danced until the late afternoon to the music of George Butts and his Hot-cross Buns. It had been an unforgettable day.

Climbing back into the Mercedes, we made our way to Laguna Beach for the first night of our honeymoon at the Surf and Sand Hotel.

CHAPTER FIFTY-TWO — WEDDING BELLS

Mr. and Mrs. Mark Ellis

I popped a champagne cork on our balcony that flew toward the surf that had surged in at high tide.

As Sally retired to the bathroom/dressing room, I reflected on my long quest to find a love that would last. Within a few months of each other, I met my bride, and I also met Jesus. Sally and I had met and dated for only a week before being separated for five months, and I almost gave up on her. Then, God answered my desperate prayer in a way that was beyond what I could have hoped or imagined.

After years of searching, I discovered that being in the heart of a divine romance was the missing piece that fulfilled my years-long quest for true love.

* * * * * *

Ellis wedding, 1985. Sally with the groomsmen.

EPILOGUE

Meeting Jesus and Sally in the same year brought profound changes into my life. It was as if one operating system had been removed from my central processor and another downloaded.

Therefore, if anyone is in Christ, he is a new creation; old things have passed away; behold, all things have become new.
—2 Corinthians 5:17 NKJV

While I once dealt poorly with the stresses and anxieties of modern life, a profound peace that goes beyond understanding filled my heart. On some level, I had feared death, but that washed away like a receding tide as I faced the future with an eternal hope.

I demonstrated the futility of my thinking and utmost selfishness in the preceding pages. I once had nothing greater to live for than burnishing my own ego, the pursuit of my own pleasures and material success. But God filled me with a higher purpose as I began to live for him.

This led to changes in my outlook about my role in the business world and, later, Christian ministry.

While I had never had much interest in reading the Bible, suddenly the words in the Bible came alive, and I had an insatiable appetite for studying Scriptures.

Finding God put me on a steady course for marriage and my future role as a father. I would have been horribly shipwrecked in both areas if I had not found faith. I have failed God many times, but His amazing grace and abundant mercies always lift me up.

He gave me the greatest gift possible, eternal life through His Son Jesus. *He who has the Son has life* ... (see 1 John 5:11-12).

* * * * * *

Mark and Sally with their first son, Sam.

ABOUT THE AUTHOR

MARK ELLIS

MARK ELLIS graduated from UC Berkeley with a degree in business administration. He worked in the commercial real estate industry for eighteen years. For nine years, he served as Assistant Pastor at Church by the Sea of Laguna Beach. He began writing about the church around the world in 1999 for *ASSIST News*.

After a trip to the southern Philippines to visit two Wycliffe Bible translators, Mark launched the God Reports website to support and encourage Christian missions. Mark is married to Sally, and they have two sons.

www.ingramcontent.com/pod-product-compliance
Lightning Source LLC
Chambersburg PA
CBHW050522170426
43201CB00013B/2047